Anger Antidotes

Anger Antidotes

HOW NOT TO LOSE YOUR S#&!

IAN BRENNAN

W. W. Norton & Company
New York • London

For information about permission to reproduce selections from this book, write to
Permissions, W. W. Norton & Company, Inc., 500 Fifth Avenue, New York, NY 10110

For information about special discounts for bulk purchases, please contact
W. W. Norton Special Sales at specialsales@wwnorton.com or 800-233-4830

Manufacturing by Malloy Printing
Book design by Jonathan Lippincott
Production manager: Leeann Graham

Library of Congress Cataloging-in-Publication Data

Brennan, Ian.
 Anger antidotes : how not to lose your S#&! / Ian Brennan.
    p. cm.
 Includes bibliographical references and index.
 ISBN 978-0-393-70705-2 (pbk.)
 1. Anger. 2. Stress management. 3. Violence. I. Title.
 BF575.A5B74 2011
 152.4'7—dc22
                        2010044405

ISBN: 978-0-393-70705-2 (pbk.)

W. W. Norton & Company, Inc.,
500 Fifth Avenue, New York, N.Y. 10110

www.wwnorton.com

W. W. Norton & Company Ltd.,
Castle House, 75/76 Wells Street, London W1T 3QT

1 2 3 4 5 6 7 8 9 0

Not "If," but "How?"
Not "Who," but "What?"
Not what we don't, but *do*, want

CONTENTS

ACKNOWLEDGMENTS

Thanks to Joan Zweben
for the support, encouragement,
and bringing me to the W. W. Norton family

This book is dedicated to
Occhi di Luce.
I never would've finished writing this
(. . . 17+ years in the making)
without your lighting the way.

PREFACE

This book is meant to be as minimal and elemental as possible. The core points are deliberately unbelabored. Rather than taking a few ideas and stretching them out over an entire book, here instead, chapters have been concentrated into "mini-manuals" that hopefully, in their totality, contain a library's worth of material.

The objective is to distill down to their most fundamental aspects the universal structures that form the basis of most human problems, both today and since time immemorial.

When we move beyond superficial differences (race, gender, age, etc.), these underlying patterns are simple to recognize and talk about, though not necessarily easy to apply and execute. More than an intellectual problem, it is our emotions that interfere with making sound choices. Thus, even the most learned individuals do "know better," but nonetheless are capable of making colossally stupid errors in judgment and conduct.

As much as we advance technologically (including the proliferation of communicational devices that, ironically, have helped accomplish little towards improving communication), we remain in the Dark Ages interpersonally, still grappling with the same basic problems and repeating near identical errors of generations past, though the inability to move beyond these limitations could in fact one day spell our end.

What follows is by no means designed to be a definitive statement on the subject of anger management or crisis resolution. Instead, the intention is to stimulate thought, confident that having the "correct" answers is best kept secondary to engaging in an ongoing exploration for truth. We all understand and "know" far more than we can articulate. The approach here is most akin to a review since almost certainly the majority of us have some expertise interpersonally (or else it'd be highly improbable that we would have made it this far). Becoming more fully conscious of our existing intuitive knowledge can simply help to reinforce and more deeply integrate it.

It is recognized that some may elect to reject all or some of the ideas put forth here. The hope is that those rejections will at least come to include an increased recognition that these types of refusals themselves still involve choice and responsibility on the part of the doer.

What follows is fashioned both for those who are struggling with their own anger as well as anyone suffering due to another's (as well as the rest of us, who are probably experiencing some combination of these factors, to varying degrees).

Personal growth need not be shrouded in mystery, available only to the educated and most privileged. It remains my conviction that any information that might aid people in their everyday functioning be as accessible to and widely-distributed as possible for all, not requiring Herculean scholarly effort to uncover and decipher.

In keeping with that, *Anger Antidotes* is written so that it can be read quite easily, cover-to-cover, during a single sitting, or randomly, in any order, and potentially be of value either way. (Additionally, central concepts recur throughout and most of them are catalogued in the brief index at the end.) Flexibility and openness to a wide variety of options are key skills for managing frustration, and hopefully the very organization of this book embodies them.

Anger Antidotes

INTRODUCTION

MEDITATIONS ON A LIFE SPENT IN THE LOONY BIN

I was baptized by the fires of anger at birth—submerged in the fury of a mentally unstable family, stretching back generations.

This life training (intensified by also having a sister with Down syndrome) led to a "make-or-be-broken" result and a set of skills well-honed for the world of emergency psychiatry (i.e., the profession that's been rated as "most dangerous" in terms of likelihood of being assaulted), where I supported myself from age 20 onwards, quite literally starting from the bottom-up—changing diapers in an unending tag-team on the nightshift of the geriatric ward, traipsing from one end of the hallway to another and then back again to re-change those who had just been cleaned. It was simultaneously back-breaking and repulsive work.

Circuitously, this led to my becoming an "expert" in verbal de-escalation and anger management, presenting an average of 200 classes per year nationwide from 1993 onwards as well as one-on-one counseling for those in trouble with the law for violence, including "celebrity" clients such as a particularly notorious former boxing champion and one of the most storied music producers of all time.

I am not of the exclusionary school that believes you have to have a "problem" with anger to understand it. Nor am I blind to the gullibility of the other extreme that imbues professionals in this area with near saint-like status and expectations. We *all* struggle and have room for improvement in the area of compassion and self control, few more so than those who stand convinced that they don't.

In the ER, raised fists, thrown chairs, threats, and brutal (often, uncannily on-target) character assassinations were the norm. In that milieu, verbal and physical abuse become taken-for-granted occupational hazards.

For years I worked with a veteran staff member on a locked ward in Oakland, California, who attempted to regale all newcomers with his extensive list of on-the-job injuries. The aim was to display his superior level of accomplishment in the field, but instead, unwittingly, all he succeeded in exposing by way of these "war stories" were his painfully obvious shortcomings.

Staying serene is not as dramatic as combat. It is much harder to brag about what *didn't* happen than what did.

Here's hoping for a quiet existence, led courageously, fully embracing the intention of "peace to all, harm to none" (. . . well, at least, *almost* none, hopefully).

PART ONE

UNIVERSAL STRUCTURES

(Please note: When the word *violence* or *violent* is used throughout this book, it is often meant to encompass the entire continuum—verbal, non-verbal, emotional, the faint and not-so-faint—and not just exclusively the blatant, physical manifestations of aggression.)

① FEAR:

THE NUCLEAR EMOTION

The core emotion, the most basic of all, and the only one necessary for survival is fear. From this emotion arises the reflexive and primordial fight-or-flight reaction (which in actuality is more accurately a fight-flight-or-*freeze* reaction).

Human beings are even *more* influenced by fear than other animals, since we are not responding just to physical threats, but also to those that are not even real or present—spiritual, emotional, verbal, psychological, or philosophical threats.

We are so ruled by these fears that we are potentially willing to die for them—to sacrifice our physical bodies in attempt to preserve or promote our egos, and ward against social death. We are even capable of killing others in the pursuit of heightening our own self-esteem. In terms of our physical survival, our superior "intelligence" makes us much dumber than other animals, which almost always choose flight as their first option and fighting only as a last resort.

Threats are exclusively the province of the threatened.

The objective is to deceive with the smoke screen, the armor of anger that conceals the underlying vulnerability. By getting the other to express fear—that which the threatener is afraid to express (i.e., the additional layer of fear: fear *of* fear)—the threatener feels temporarily powerful and less afraid. But self-defeatingly, the threatener's own threatening behavior causes others to bolster their counterattacks and, ultimately, the net-effect is even greater fright.

(Note: One of the more profound proofs that fear underlies anger is that in multiple studies, childhood bullies steadfastly identify those with neutral facial expressions as being "mean" and/or "not liking" them.)

Ironically, so much dishonorable behavior comes as a result of people striving to "defend their honor."

a) Loss Aversion

Statistically, we are much more motivated by what we can lose than what we can gain.

This perspective keeps us locked in a past-oriented, conservative mode whereby we potentially repeat and compound our own errors. Las Vegas is founded on this basic tendency (e.g., once we've lost some money, most of us will usually continue to invest even more in the quest to regain what has already been squandered).

It is routinely much better to be proactive and deny something at the outset rather than later take from someone what they feel is already rightly theirs based on a precedent. The potency of ownership is why individuals are customarily very flexible with where they will sit in a group upon first arriving somewhere, but once settled and established, are very resistant to and irritated by *then* having to move (from a space that they feel they've now taken as theirs).

Most people are open at the outset, but once a pact or promise is made, they will resist any movement backwards, tooth-and-nail.

Many even live most of their lives based on "what ifs," allowing highly unlikely outcomes to overshadow their every decision (e.g., "But 'what if' you take that new job and then the company goes bankrupt?"; etc.), and thus any change, even a seemingly positive one, invites tremendous apprehension.

Antidote

Fundamentally, humans are in need of affirmation (to be seen and understood) and reassurance (that they are alright *and* that everything else will be, as well). Though not easy to achieve, if they can reach a point of acknowledging the imperfection of the universe, thereafter those individuals become potentially better able to accept when something is not working as it *should* and acquiesce sooner, rather than compounding their error by devoting ever more intensity to the tact that they are already pursuing (i.e., the hallmark of superficial versus true, paradigm-shifting change), or their insistence in renouncing whatever actually *is*.

Pressure can be eased by framing interactions in noncompetitive ways so that individuals do not see reality, or every less-than-ideal outcome, as a "defeat."

b) The Myth of Scarcity

Fear drives people to become emotional misers.

The paranoid belief that there is only a limited amount of love or good fortune to go around causes people to view one another defensively and contentiously.

What this tendency belies is the fact that we almost always receive back whatever it is that we have given out—if we smile, we are more likely to be smiled at, and if we strike others, we are more likely to eventually be struck ourselves (i.e., a common-sense truth that has been officially proven in study after study).

Antidote

Rather than "losing" what we offer, we almost invariably have it returned to us, in multiples. When endeavoring to balance the books of human interaction (an almost impossible task, to begin with), it is helpful if we take into consideration not just what is immediately happening, but the more far-reaching net effect of our efforts.

② BEHAVIORAL CONTAGION

Behavior is contagious.

If one person laughs, others are more likely to do so as well. And as these effects are amplified, the larger the audience and collective proof.

Just like we can catch a cough, we can catch someone's attitude.

A prime objective is to resist being infected by ill behavior, and instead, "cure" the other through our maintenance of self control. This is almost always achieved by exercising choice.

Control is the crossroads of crisis.

It is very difficult to escalate emotionally in the presence of someone who is remaining calm . . . it is not at all an easy task to argue with someone who is agreeing with you . . . and it is more than challenging to blame someone who has proven him- or herself above reproach (i.e., due to that person's having overperformed).

It is almost impossible to "fight with" someone who is not fighting back. What was designed to be "fair" and "just" exchange with meritorious outcome, suddenly is exposed for the butchery it really is. We cannot teach someone that fighting is wrong by counterattacking them; we teach them that fighting is wrong by not rewarding their motives with the conduct and aims they seek.

Violence is a Pandora's Box.

Once the chasm is crossed from impulse to action, peace is never quite fully restored. Even in victory, the threat of retaliation, stemming from the longing for revenge, lingers.

The cycle of attack–counterattack is only broken when one or both parties ceases being violent. Unfortunately, this usually only occurs involuntarily—through death, substantial injury, or restraint (e.g., incarceration). "What goes around, comes around" keeps a Ferris Wheel of retribution in perpetual motion.

On a strictly legal level, it is worth noting that often the attention of witnesses is attracted only after the fact, so all that they see is the counterattack, which in their account is "what happened."

Antidote

In general, we should strive to speak more quietly than the person with whom we are speaking. Nearly without fail, people lose self control first *vocally* then *verbally* then *physically*—and when they become physical, they usually stop talking at all.

By erring on the side of doing less rather than more, we help compensate for the reality that in crisis situations, most of us are exhibiting far more vigor than we realize.

Control yourself, and you control the world (i.e., at least, your own "personal empire"). Attempt to control the world, and inevitably in time you will be controlled.

When someone challenges us with a fight-flight-or-freeze situation, the most suitable response is actually to do neither. Instead, we can defend without retaliation, using only necessary force, undeterred in our pursuit of a win–win outcome.

The fundamental question would best be: are we fighting destructively over the past (which we cannot undo or change) or constructively for the future (which we still might be able to influence)?

Possible pitfall: A common trap is confusing apathy with self control. Apathy may be less obviously provocative, but it is still extreme—a vacuum—and therefore potentially troublesome. With empathy, which is inherent in self control, emotion is not absent, just regulated.

③ ASYMMETRICAL REVENGE

Reciprocity is the global currency of human inter-action.

You smile, I smile (this is a hard-wired reflex, one of the first to materialize in infancy). You say hello, I'm supposed to greet you back. Failure to do so can even be construed by some as an act of war.

When brought into the antisocial arena, this pattern results in the escalation of an "eye for an eye, a tooth for a tooth." What this oft-recited bit of folk-wisdom fails to reflect accurately, though, is that it is not actually an "eye for an eye," but instead more akin to "a *head* for an eye." The receiver will almost always do something worse than what was done to him or her.

The psychological source of this tendency is documented in studies where most people minimize or deny whatever wrongs they have committed, but almost always overestimate and exaggerate whatever was done *to them*.

One person may have indeed started it, but it almost always takes two to finish it. Similarly, most accidents occur when not one, but *two* bad drivers intersect (e.g., the first running a red light while the other is looking down at their phone, thus, being unable to compensate for the first person's error as they would otherwise under more balanced circumstances), while most catastrophes arise from a clash between two poles—a preternaturally naïve person happening upon a notably sinister one—or when two people's value systems are completely cross-wired (e.g., one party who doesn't think that being punctual is a "big deal" arriving at a meeting with another for whom lateness is their foremost annoyance).

Sadly, people often are more likely to *respond in hate* (which they may feel obliged to address), than to *respond in kind* (which they may feel is permissible to ignore). In any retaliation, we risk "becoming the 'enemy,'" even though ostensibly the aspiration is to inspire the other to become more like us (e.g., hopefully it is the confident parent that is modeling for the tantrumming child and not the other way around).

Antidote

Our calm can short-circuit the automatic behavior matching and amplification process.

The provoker seeks the antagonizer's negative behavior. Without it, it is very difficult for the provoker to make the case that he or she has been wronged and that the other is deserving of punishment.

Almost all violent individuals believe that they are victims. As noted above, they focus selectively on whatever the other did, while denying or disregarding their own participation. This deliberate blindness enables them to assign blame in an absolute, all-or-nothing manner.

It's an age-old truth that prison walls are filled almost exclusively with convicted "victims"—victims of circumstances, victims of the system, victims of *every*thing. Most of all though, as much as they may refuse to admit it, they are victims of themselves.

They are not blameless in the way they would like others to believe, but they do remain perpetual victims of their own strict codes of conduct and perfectionistic visions, which rob them of choices and creativity, leaving them at the mercy of chance and their environment (and haunted by the basic guilt and shame that they, too, have not been enough).

Rather than serving as a green light for fury (e.g., to the person who seeks "warranted" and welcomed occasions to vent), crisis better serves as a red light to slow down and be extra mindful.

(4) MORAL CALCULUS

The failure of most when calculating the math of interpersonal dealings is that they use simple addition: They match whatever it is that the other is doing. By doing so, we simply create *more* of what we purportedly don't want (e.g., two people yelling instead of just one).

Whether or not you want to "take shit" from others, they are going to *give it*. What you do with it is where the "thought of least resistance" (i.e., primitive, overly simplified conclusions) can be held at bay, and the elements of choice and control are brought more fully into play.

Antidote

When choice rather than ideals is accentuated, we remain empowered, *even* in less-than-perfect circumstances. It can be helpful to vigil that we, and not our surroundings, are dictating our responses, and that choices are not being censored by what we think we "can't" do.

If we are genuinely striving for constructive outcomes, our objective needs to be more intricate than merely matching the other's behavior. The task is to bridge, rather than compound, the deficit by *doing whatever it is that the other person is not*—but probably should be—*doing*. On a transactional level, we are giving them a short-term, good-faith loan to bridge the current shortfall.

We are not likely to solve an interaction with an immature individual by acting as (or more) immaturely than him or her. Resolution comes through our behaving *more* maturely than him or her (and, in essence, performing both for ourselves *and* on the other person's behalf, too). With someone who is not speaking, we must work even harder at the communication, not less. And if someone is irrational, we must be more rational to compensate.

Macho ethics encourage gambling, with the stakes being our own life, safety, or freedom. Conversely, the question that would consummately frame all of our encounters could be: Is this trivial moment worth *that* exorbitant of a price?

With astonishingly grim injuries, physical or otherwise, there truly may be no penalty or compensation that is high enough to repay the debt anyway. No matter how many countless people may be punished or killed, a loved one will still never be brought back from the dead, nor a wrong undone (instead, it will merely be *re*-done, by us).

The challenge is not one of being decent to the pleasant people, for almost anyone can do that. The true accomplishment is being kind to the difficult ones.

To "*not* do unto others as they do to you."

⑤ EMOTIONAL IMMATURITY

Human folly almost always results from one thing: emotional immaturity. It is not from intellectual or informational deficits that most evil usually originates, as is often presumed. Emotions play a part in our decision-making processes and often override intellect.

As a vivid example, when studying the three roles (perpetrator, follower/bystander, rescuer) individuals fall into during acts of genocide, there is found only one characteristic that distinguishes them from each other: emotional maturity. Not surprisingly, the more violent are the least mature, and the protectors, the most, by a wide margin.

On a neurological level, the emotional part of the brain is triggered three times more quickly than the intellect. That means that our consciousness is constantly playing a game of catch-up, trying to revise or justify the "decision-making" process.

Audience members are rarely entirely innocent. Though they may be passive and presume that they "weren't involved," they are still part of the system and participating. Their presence alone alters the tenor of a circumstance, and the support and/or validation of spectators often acts as an inflammatory catalyst for action that otherwise might not have happened. In worst-case scenarios, the third party surreptitiously or unconsciously goads someone else to act out for him or her (e.g., the sexually stymied parent who sexualizes his or her child so that the parent can then live through them vicariously).

The moral slide into genocide is often initiated through a coercive twist on "kill or be killed" with perpetrators limiting bystanders to that dreadful choice—you kill them or we'll kill *you*. Not surprisingly, the use of drugs and alcohol is almost always present as well as a lubricant in altering the population's sensibilities (with initial recruits generally made up of orphaned and impoverished adolescent males who frequently, also, already hold personal grudges towards the scapegoated group due to prior violence where they and/or their own family members were the victims.

Violence often is an act of perfectionistic, obsessive compulsion that feeds the attempt to rid the world of all undesirable elements, in an insatiable expansion (i.e., one aspect being eliminated or controlled will never be good enough since through this process, new, previously tolerated problems that then need to be "fixed," too, will inevitably arise, rewidening the void of this unfinishable quest).

Antidote

With more value placed on knowing what we feel rather than what we "think"—or, worse yet, *denial* of what we feel (i.e., the most basic of defense mechanisms)—we can potentially assume increased responsibility for our own conduct and explore a broader range of options for resolution.

"That's probably true (in *some* ways)," is a mantra of nondefensiveness that can be used as response to almost any opinion that one encounters.

⑥ ECONOMICS OF ENERGY

Ultimately, truly objective evaluations consider one criterion: Is what is being done creating the desired result?

Whether what we are doing "should" be succeeding or is the "right" thing to do is of little help when we are faced with its ineffectiveness. Whatever "it" is may very well have worked in the past, but the current circumstance is all that is in our immediate realm of influence.

In terms of assessment, bedrock is whether what we are doing is successful. Is the situation getting better or worse? Very rarely will things remain neutral following our involvement.

If what we are doing is not functioning as planned, flexibility and curiosity can aid us in exploring and creating options whose exclusion might otherwise leave us trapped in a helpless state.

Antidote

Stubbornly waiting for the world to change is futile, but exercising our capabilities to relate and adjust to the world can, paradoxically, modify situations themselves.

Actions not only take, but *give*, energy. Rather than simply estimating the initial output costs of an activity, the emotional and spiritual "expense" of an experience—whether it is inspirational (i.e., invigorating and energy-giving) or dispiriting (i.e., draining and energy-stealing), might better be tallied.

All energy is not expended equally. Some energy we gladly exert, other energies—begrudgingly so. For example, we have an amazing ability to find ways to overcome almost all obstacles when in pursuit of something that is attractive to us—in which cases we might even drive more than 200 miles, after working a double shift, to see our favorite sports team or musical group or someone we truly love and cherish. In contrast is the near-paralysis that can occur when faced with even the tiniest but most dreaded of tasks—such as taking out the trash or paying bills. This is why many very successful people advise doing whatever you loathe first, to clear the way and create momentum towards the easier and more appealing things. The sense of misery resulting from leaving the worst till last can siphon off oxygen from all other surrounding activities and leave us lifeless.

If we truly have encountered someone who is so insulated and unbending that "nothing works," then from that point forward we should more or less do just that: nothing. The use of extinction (i.e., ceasing or minimizing all contact, such as refusing to make even the briefest of eye contact with a street hustler) is the equivalent of closing the door to a room where a fire has broken out so that the flames are contained and aren't fed by oxygen. There is no real sense in speaking unless someone is listening or, even worse, has proven able and determined to twist our each and every olive branch offered into ammunition for continuing their tirade campaign.

⑦ PROACTIVITY:

THE INVISIBLE LABOR

Opportunity dictates action.

Opportunity forms the gateway whereby impulses and temptation are rallied. For example, one is more likely to relapse at a hosted bar than while sitting in services at a tee-totaler church.

What differentiates us from animals is the ability to stop and think before we act (. . . or don't act). When we do this, what we are thinking about specifically are the imagined future consequences of the action we are considering.

This ability to pause and think (which often occurs in seconds or fraction of seconds) creates the choices that empower us to respond and not simply react to transient situational factors. Few haven't had their "buttons pushed" at times. In that state we expectedly have reduced say-so as to whether we respond (or don't), and we can effectively end up on "autopilot."

The fewer the hurdles to a desired goal (be it an achievement, access to a person, a possession, or an event), the greater the temptation to move forward towards that goal, and the more a behavior is potentiated or energized. And if we underestimate or deny the danger in those risky situations to which we are drawn—that is, if we don't think carefully before we leap (perhaps literally) into action—we court possibilities that would otherwise be less of a factor. (Note: Almost whenever the pursuit or enacting of certain desires is made more private—for example, easy and free access to pornography on the Internet—the behavior commensurately proliferates.)

Big or small, we are constantly managing and being influenced by opportunity, be it a dog on a leash, a prison's construction, the tendency towards duplicity of multilingual individuals when in the presence of a monolingualist (i.e., talking "behind their back"—or more accurately right in front of their face—not because they are more apt to do so, but simply because they are more *able*), or our devouring things on an airplane that we would never consider ingesting otherwise.

Antidote

"An ounce of prevention is worth a pound of cure." By making small and preemptive efforts to block the openings where crises manifest (e.g., fastening a seat belt, not jaywalking, locking our doors and windows), a sizable bulk of "victimizations" are eliminated. And these preemptive efforts would not be possible without our ability to contemplate before we act.

Those who "live dangerously," "flirt with disaster," or "ask for trouble" are more likely to suffer dire consequences as a result. Mature courage involves taking minimal, available steps to protect others from being penalized in the aftermath of *our* unnecessary recklessness; to rebel responsibly, as it were. People would best be held accountable not only for their actively inappropriate antics, but also for the severe endangerment that occurs when a modicum of adequate caution and/or care is not taken.

A good technique related to this is to become more aware of energy paths—where something is or could be headed, physically or emotionally. Whether it is an acquaintance who possibly has unwelcome romantic intentions, the direction a sharp knife is pointed after we have set it on the kitchen counter, or the area directly in front of and within arm's reach of another (where almost every hand-to-hand assault in history has and will ever occur), it is usually best to not position ourselves in these locations to begin with.

More than avoiding "being in the wrong place at the wrong time," even better yet is to err on the side of caution and rarely be there at all, as much as we can avoid it. Though we may feel the right thing to do is "stand and fight," most martial arts experts advise that even if our loved ones are being held, *even then* we should still choose flight (i.e., running to get help) if possible. We cannot aid anyone if we are incapacitated through injury, and almost no one gains from our getting injured, *including* the person who injures us (who is likely to later suffer consequences because of it).

When are we ever *not* managing crisis to some degree? Even the most routine situation, if handled insensitively enough, can escalate. The best crisis intervention—prevention—often goes uncredited.

The suggestion is not that we should tiptoe through the world on eggshells while ensconced in bubble-wrap. The crux of the matter is developing the poise to engage in risk-reduction, yet still robustly experience "life" (i.e., to find some balance between two extremes).

⑧ PSYCHOLOGICAL PRIMING:

NOT-*SO*-GREAT EXPECTATIONS

What we expect to happen is largely what will happen (in our perception, at any rate).

Those who are negatively primed to find fault and see the bad rather than good, not surprisingly suffer from greater anger and depression. Expectations act as kindling for impudence since so much ire is triggered by a sense of disappointment or having been treated unfairly. If things going the way they "should" operates as our gauge for whether or not to explode, then we had better stand braced for a lifetime of pyrotechnics.

Expectations can cut both ways. When too extreme of an estimate is made, there can be a backlash, whereby the good or bad is scrutinized more severely. For example, if someone tells another how terrific a restaurant or movie is, that person will almost certainly be more disposed to like it. But if that recommendation is way off the mark and overly subjective, it can boomerang and something that might otherwise have been seen neutrally is suddenly cast as "surprisingly good" or "shockingly bad."

Many cross-cultural conflicts result, at least in part, from the respective bias of each (neutral, positive, negative) that colors the interpretation of another's actions (e.g., whether a stranger bumping into us was "on purpose," an accident, or merely an occurrence that transpires completely unnoticed).

Antidote

The Principle of Contrasts influences our opinions. If we have prepared someone for the possibility or likelihood of "the worst" (preferably, as early as we can, before that person has really begun to form a different idea), then any improvement on that forecast is likely to be received favorably even though it might still fall very short of his or her ideal.

After a salesperson informs us that that a "good" suit costs at minimum $2,500, a $399 one suddenly might seem quite reasonable and "cheap," even though it far exceeds what we'd originally planned to pay. Similarly, a 6-foot person can look rather "short" while standing on court next to professional basketball players.

This phenomenon of contrasts can work in our favor, as our kindness and composure will almost always exist in sharp distinction to the all-too-common unsympathetic conduct that most frustrated, relationally-handicapped individuals encounter. Being truly listened to or identified with is a vital need, but one that is seldom met. The sad truth is, most people we encounter (as well as possibly ourselves) are starved for compassion.

It is advisable to have clarity from the start, rather than trying to trick someone into going along with a course of action by gambling with his or her expectations, such that he or she then might experience the shock later that the entire endeavor was founded on false pretenses or a "misunderstanding." It behooves us to do our best to not overlook opportunities for understanding (which often entail identifying and empathizing with the other's emotional state), whenever and wherever they may present themselves. A little effort can go a long way in this regard.

Over and above problem-solving, we can pursue an ongoing solution-*formation* mode whereby strife-free intervals are seen as the anomaly (the opposite of a "pie-in-the-sky" belief system), with adaptation and compromise instead being held as the norms.

⑨ INVOLUNTARY RELATIONSHIPS

Modern life is largely composed of involuntary relationships, through which we are forced to interact with people—usually strangers—that we did not choose and that, typically, did not choose us either. Be they coworkers, customers and/or clerks in a retail setting, or fellow public-transit travelers, the list can go on and on.

a) Confusing Social with Asocial

When social models (i.e., being "nice" with the expectation that niceness will be returned) are misapplied to *a*social encounters—that is, a transient relationship based on intersecting, immediate goals, such as my being an employee at a café so that I can receive money for serving you coffee and your entering the café to be served coffee by a stranger for the cash you give—the preexisting problems in the structure of the relationship are only exacerbated.

Contrary to pop-psychology "wisdom," these types of relationships actually *are* transactional and conditional (and, like it or lump it, they comprise the bulk of our day-to-day contacts).

Antidote

Instead of focusing on "who" (the "you/I"—social model)—one can focus on "what"—the asocial task at hand that unites us temporarily.

If this were truly a relationship founded on "who," the reality is that in many cases the relationship would not exist in the first place. On a fundamental level, one of us would be fighting or fleeing, or at least not persisting. If we keep our focus on the task at hand—be it paying for our groceries or getting safely to our destination—we can sidestep the social quagmires that might arise if we were to take a more social, personal focus.

Possible pitfall: One of the more common confusions is who is working for whom, whereby the employed treats the customer as if they are instead working for them (e.g., adopting a condescending and/or irritable tone in response to appropriate and nominal requests for information). In an era of self-appointed pseudo-experts about virtually everything, it remains even more vital that we not lose sight that all employment is based on the same single, rudimentary behavioral contract whereby the worker willingly agrees to suspend and subordinate most of his or her own needs for "x" number of hours in exchange for "x" amount of cash. Even in the most drastic cases of a police officer arresting or physically apprehending someone, that officer is still, in fact, working on behalf of the citizens, *including* the person that is being taken into police custody.

b) The Intimacy of Violence

When an act of violence occurs, an intimate bond is inadvertently forged between the attacker and victim, or co-attacker (the latter, in the case of mutual combat). Literally, the victim or co-attacker becomes the most important person in the world at that moment, someone for whom the attacking person is willing to kill or die and risk all for (career, reputation, finances). The two (or more) participants' destinies become potently merged, possibly in an irreversible way.

Due to viewing the world in a crude and unrestrained way, perfectionists in particular struggle with inappropriate, random overtures and are susceptible to aggression because they lack proportion and so are often unable to be selective about who they engage or don't. In essence, their perfectionism places them under the spell of their environment and chance, and leaves them little choice about whom they allow into their lives. For them, those who otherwise could remain anonymous instead cannot be refused, and thus relationships are mandated and fated since all invitations received must be accepted (e.g., the perfectionistic father accompanying his toddler to the park and ending up in a physical altercation with a drunk "scumbag" that he'd never met before . . . and probably never *would have* again).

Oftentimes, attackers will describe their victims by stating that they "didn't deserve to live," yet they themselves are willing to throw away their *own* lives over someone whom they've deemed as worthless, a subtext that potentially reveals so much about the dynamics of "fighting."

Antidote

Rather than rejecting those closest to us in favor of an impulsive "fling" with a stranger, it serves us well to place those we love between us and any devious third party (including addictions and other temptations). If we are not able to act judiciously on behalf of ourselves, we hopefully can at least do so out of concern for our beloved.

What those we hate or are apathetic to might think can only pale to irrelevancy when juxtaposed with the protection of those and that which we adore. Our "*self* defense" involves people far beyond us and those immediately present, and when compromised, it can resonate throughout families and communities with the devastation of an earthquake followed by aftershocks for many years (or even generations) to come.

The core question is, "Do we want to have a relationship at all with this stranger? (or up the intensity with this acquaintance)?" If we have to ask at all, the answer, almost always, is likely to be an irrefutable "no."

⑩ *OTHER*-CENTEREDNESS:
REACHING BEYOND THE SELF

Since involuntary relationships are unavoidable, it seems almost indisputable that techniques for dealing with them can potentially have benefit.

In the context of stressful circumstances, the other can most accurately be viewed not as an adversary, but, instead, as our ally. We are in this—albeit, less than ideal—relationship together. And, the compensatory steps we can take are not only beneficial to us, but to them as well.

a) Right or Wrong *Is* Wrong

Moral judgments are of little help in trying situations. No matter how wrong someone might be, odds are that they are convinced that they are right.

The more we attack their position as wrong, the more self-righteous and recalcitrant they will usually become, as well as the more convinced that *we* are "wrong."

It is an unwinnable debate whether or not we are good people or care or understand what others are experiencing. If they believe that we are prejudiced against them, its being "true" or not becomes insignificant. If they *feel* that they are correct, then that feeling will be the operant factor—the driver—of their behavior.

Antidote

By placing our desire to understand the other ahead of our own need to be understood, energies are devoted to communication rather than contest.

The more we ask "What?", the more precise the other will usually become. This is the concept of "laddering" whereby we keep asking "what" as a way of achieving greater specificity and digging more deeply into what the individual is actually feeling and motivated by—the emotion beneath the behavior, the emotion *beneath* the emotion.

Much violence results from self-centered interpretations that can eventually lead to outlandish conclusions, like "That (blind) guy was staring at me" or "I really told that (deaf) dude off for ignoring me." It tends to work best for us to, at the very least, encourage ourselves to try and consider the other person's possible perception (or lack thereof) and experience—that is, whatever non-obvious or out-of-the-norm factors might be influencing him or her currently.

b) You *Are* "Right," Nothing Will Work *All* of the Time

So far we have emphasized that things are rarely, if ever, absolute.

What we can better focus on are the commonalities, the things that are more prevalent and most often apply.

Exceptions to the rules *do* exist. That is why they are exceptional (e.g., the person who persists or escalates even when our responses have been by-the-book and exemplary).

Sad, but true, there are some people for whom, no matter how much we try to do "the right thing," it will still be wrong (in fact, in many cases, it may get worse the more we try). If a person is angered enough there may be nothing we can possibly say that is "right."

Antidote

By surrendering and accepting our own powerlessness, we actually empower others to take responsibility for themselves and reduce or eliminate blame, so that they, conversely, assume at least some fractional ownership of their own conduct.

It would be difficult to identify a more unintentionally revealing statement regarding a person's sense of frailty and impotence than when that person, if angered, claims that he or she was "made" to do something (e.g., "You make me so crazy"; "You pissed me off"; "I had no choice but to tell him off").

A goal is to surrender to complex and varied outlooks by acknowledging that whatever is being stated *could* be true (in *some* way).

⑪ MOTIVATIONS

Though we might not always be able to identify, or will misidentify, our own motives, all behavior has a causal origin and endeavors to meet some need. Unfortunately, often the very opposite result from that which we desire is elicited from the world.

a) The Quest for Respect

A primary currency in human interaction is respect.

Secure people possess a self-respect that fulfills the bulk of their needs and eases their reliance on others for those needs to be met.

Insecure individuals frequently exhibit their most disrespectful antics when starving or striving for respect, which sets in motion a downwardly-spiraling negative feedback loop—by which, the more they need respect, the less they get.

Antidote

It is usually better to *show*, via sincere attention and listening, than *tell* others what we feel about them. The more we try to convince others how we feel—for example, that we "admire" them—the more likely it is to become an improvable factual contention.

For those in distress, demonstrations of respect almost always occur at exchange rates that favor the seller—what we give out has worth far beyond its normal "market value"—since those that crave it value it more than those who don't.

And who better to supply those much-needed commodities to ourselves than *our*selves—thereby cutting out the middleman. For example, my core self-worth—the appreciation that I have value independent of the results that I produce—preferably would remain more or less the same before and after a business meeting, no matter what the outcome.

b) Meaning-Making

The "oxygen" of the psyche is meaning. The brain is in an ongoing state of processing experiences (crude data) and shaping them into meaning (output). When we witness an unusual behavior or experience a tragedy, we usually feel almost beholden to try to figure out a "reason" why it happened.

In serving this process, whether a given conclusion is accurate or not stands secondary to its being formed and filed. Once an opinion is solidified (through the web of associations from stored images), past orientation joins in, motoring it further down the line until it becomes almost irrefutable. Things become derailed when the conclusion that's reached lacks objective logic, with each error of this sort potentially leading to more and even greater ones.

Antidote

Recognizing the myopic trap of narcissism, which so often produces illogic and subjectivity, can serve as a caution to not make too much out of any isolated incident solely because we were the ones to have directly experienced it, but that could actually prove misrepresentative of any overall pattern. For example, "That's not what *I* heard" is the narrow refrain of a past orientation that casts whatever comes first as incontestably correct while also ascribing the self as the supreme informational source (e.g., a person who trusts too blindly in their own finite field of knowledge).

Actively looking for the counterweight of "exceptions to the rule" helps keep us open to possibility and new or revised outlooks.

One of the best methods for ascertaining what another might be feeling is to instead examine whatever it is that *we* are feeling, which often acts as a mirror. For example, manipulative individuals tend to frustrate others, which is what they themselves will not admit but usually are experiencing—frustration. Intimidating individuals want to make others afraid, because that is the emotion that they fear most to experience, let alone express.

Possible pitfall: Adrenaline acts as a fixative on the brain. Therefore, whatever experience comes coupled with it—whether negative or pleasurable—will make a larger, potentially overshadowing impression, particularly if it is novel (e.g., our first time doing almost anything).

c) Emotion-Centric

No matter how much thought is involved, almost all action remains irrational (e.g., "I know it's probably a bad idea, *but* . . . "). We are driven by emotion.

It can be argued that all deeds and purchases seek the same basic product: contentment. Whether one buys a car, goes out for an expensive dinner, or takes a vacation halfway around the world, all are ultimately pursuing the same objective: to feel good or, *at least*, better, even when the long-term impact of our action deepens the agony (e.g., the alcoholic who might be at peace for a moment while drinking, but ultimately feels even worse afterwards).

Antidote

The more that we are nourished nonmaterially (i.e., internally), the more self-sustaining we become and thus, less vulnerable to outside influence. Cravings for experiences and things (i.e., the means) are best relinquished in place of nourishing the underlying feeling that they serve (i.e., the end result that those means fulfill).

Exercising "mind over matter" can be helpful because the body is an extension of, and serves, the mind. Without the mind's participation, most experiences lack meaning and, in fact, go unrecognized and/or unfelt. For all intents and purposes, they have not happened (e.g., if we were to sever select nerves to the brain, one could set one's own arm on fire and feel nothing).

Without the presence of something positive, negatives easily enter to fill the void (as in the adage, "Idle hands are the Devil's playthings"). From boredom can arise obsession with every sensation, which during more structured periods would hardly register. The next time we feel ourselves starting to become sick or getting irritated, it can be beneficial to choose to refuse to allow the illness or emotion to progress further (though not ignoring it *entirely* either). Rather than the brain being seized by the body's every whim, it is helpful to exercise the brain's power of selection. Many people become "sick" or get in trouble when they have "nothing better to do," are ravenous for interest from others, or feel unable to ask for help otherwise (i.e., overdriven perfectionists). Yet, ironically, experts identify a key to longevity is *our* maintaining interest in the world, one of the reasons that is identified as to why photographers and painters often live such long lives, since they spend so much of their time looking (and looking very intently) at the world.

Those who are dissociated from their emotions are especially prone to inflict self-harm in order to try to give expression and source to their malaise (e.g., people who self-cut in an effort to either feel something/*any*thing at all or to try and help identify "where" their existential pain is coming from).

A good practice is that anytime something goes "wrong," instead of seething, employ it as a cue to be thankful that things are not so much worse. As bad as things get, as long as we are still alive, we have some reason to be potentially content and we have, at minimum, some guarded hope for the future— that is, that in time there could be a comparative, if not complete, improvement.

PART TWO

RECURRING CAUSES

⑫ THE ABSENCE OF THOUGHT

The universal reflexive question people ask when attempting to make sense of an abhorrent action—What was he [or she] thinking?—is, pardon the bluntness, an essentially stupid inquiry.

The answer is, they were *not* thinking. That's why they did what they did. If they had been thinking, they probably would've done something else, or at least less momentous, than what actually ensued.

Corroboration of these cognitive deficits is found ad nauseam in worldwide crime data that documents how alcohol or drugs are involved in the staggering majority of rapes, murders, and assaults.

Antidote

We can *potentially* stimulate rational thought in another through two main means:

1. *Asking questions*: In order to answer a question, the other person first must think. Even if he chooses not to speak, he still must pause, however briefly, to consider whether or not to reply. If he does speak, he becomes the "barking dog that doesn't bite"—since engaging in verbal behavior is usually incompatible with assault (i.e., most people will stop speaking before or while physically attacking another).

2. *Giving options*: Providing choices places the individual in a decision-making role. In order to make a decision, she must first think and contemplate the choices. Additionally, this process empowers the individual, counteracting her sense of constriction and powerlessness by focusing on solutions and that which *is* possible, which enlists her in a leadership role.

⑬ EMOTIONAL INTOXICATION & INCONTINENCE

Few benefit from loss of self control. Those who suffer most are often the ones who have "lost it."

Our anger is *our* problem, usually troubling us much more than anyone else who we might mistakenly believe caused it by "making" us angry. People can almost never make us do anything that we don't choose to do ourselves. They can, in severe cases, present us with terribly bad choices (e.g., get in the car or be shot), but almost always some element of choice remains ours.

Anger is self-generated. We don't feel angry as much as "get angry." *We* make ourselves angry based on how we interpret our experiences. The angrier we get, the angrier we become. We literally get better at it through practice, building neural pathways in the process in the same manner a pianist or basketball star does for their respective arts. Rage-proneness is closely linked to rumination and brooding, the unwillingness to forgive and let go (i.e., past orientation)—not just getting mad, but *staying* mad.

It is truly involuntary whether we bleed or not if we are attacked physically, but with verbal, emotional, and psychological assaults, we *do* have the ability and luxury to lessen, alter, or even reverse their impact.

When we "lose control" of ourselves, we almost invariably lose far more as a result.

These interpersonal outbursts can have far-ranging consequences, not just diminishing future opportunities, but also retroactively and negatively revising past achievements. For example, a person could be "happily" married for 50 years and if in one impulsive microsecond during a spat throws a plate and accidentally kills his spouse, almost all of the goodwill that has come before is negated, in that single instant.

The assertion "I can be a real asshole when I have to be" is hardly a badge of honor. And the rationale "He can be nice" is an all-but-irrelevant defense, as even those capable of the greatest evil *can* be and *are* nice *some* of the time to *some* people.

Antidote

The psychological trapdoors and escape clauses of "if," "unless," and "but" leave one playing a treacherous game of Russian roulette with reality. For our own benefit, commitments to self control should be ironclad and without contingency plans for bad conduct.

Irresistible urges are a fabrication. Even in the heat of passion people can exercise traces of self control and discretion (e.g., compulsive serial killers have been found more than able to restrain themselves if police officers are present and a likelihood of being apprehended is high).

These internal contracts are best made far in advance of any stimulus, so that if we ever do encounter the misfortune of being tested in some unexpected flash—during which the course of our existence could needlessly change due to an unfortunate convergence between our self-image, society's standards, and the sloppy mess of actuality—we can *choose* to *respond* rather than *react* and prevent being dictated to and victimized by our circumstances.

Damaging individuals are mistaken as to what to hold sacred, and, consequently, take up trivial crusades (i.e., ego) in lieu of truly noble causes (e.g., protection of others). The application of non-negotiable "can't/have/shoulds" is best reserved for those very rare and globally-unified conventions (e.g., not lying; not deliberately harming others), and otherwise discarded.

We are never *not* communicating. Though we may speak little or not at all, emotion is still being conveyed. The reflexive defense of "I didn't do anything" translates into "I didn't *say* anything" (i.e., in denial of the fact that doing "nothing" *is* still "doing something").

Those who rely too heavily on words (i.e., are "up in their heads") are, for all purposes, "blind" through their other sensory channels. These one-trick ponies are practically unable to detect or express certain elements. Think of the intellectual who is so divorced from her own face and body that she appears almost paralyzed and often seems as if performing a recitation when speaking since the primary concern is with what is being "said."

Underlying (and underlining or contradicting) anything we say—or don't say—is what we express.

Almost all formal laws of society are based on restricting only two channels of communication: verbal (words) and haptic (touch).

Due to this legal configuration, all but the most out-of-control individuals will consciously or unconsciously manage these two modes to the best of their ability, going through the motions and making

Abuses tend to occur by way of the other three accessible channels: proxemics (use of interpersonal space), kinesics (body and facial expressions), and paraverbal cues (the vocal features of how we say what we are saying—the rate, rhythm, pitch, tone). As long as I don't "say" the wrong thing, I can "get away with murder" through the other three channels. For example, I can refuse to look at someone while assuring him that "Everything is okay"; or, I can let out a loud, deep, unrestrained sigh or yawn while sitting through a lecture or class. In a myriad of ways, I can say what's required while still conveying my actual (and even contradictory) experience of a situation via the silent language of the body.

Physical aggression *is* in fact a form of communication. Some would argue it is our first dialogue with the world (e.g., a toddler decidedly tossing aside something it finds distasteful). Energy is the universal language of all living things. Though, like with any language, it is not understood infallibly; we emerge as infants with some ability to communicate in this manner (e.g., a dog has a fairly good sense of whether we are afraid of it or not, with or without the aid of intellect).

Antidote

Nature is energy-conservative and fundamentally self-correcting in its hunt for equilibrium. The feedback we receive almost always has a seed of truth in what it reflects. It is madness to suppose that it is the world that is wrong and we who are unwaveringly right. What can be wise is to periodically suss out and soften the ethical blind spots that almost all of us may have, and which are often remnants of bad models from childhood (e.g., having picked up on our caretakers' unhealthy habits or prejudices).

History is almost always smarter than we are. What an individual has done before is the single most reliable predictor of future behavior. The difference between having done something once and never is immense. The significance of having done something twice instead of just once is enormous—since it all but eliminates the slim chance that the behavior before was isolated and situational, establishing instead that there is a pattern. Additionally, repetition tends to be more provocative to others. Most people will tolerate initial trespasses, but are liable to become much less forgiving with each recurrence (e.g., the postman gets bit because he or she keeps going back).

The longer the time has passed since any behavior has occurred, the less significant it tends to be (e.g., almost everyone has committed at least minor acts of aggression in childhood and/or adolescence, yet these rarely are relevant to their adult life).

The exact interval that parallel sociological disciplines have consistently found as the pivot point when long-term damage occurs—be it irreversible combat trauma or the presence of a chronic mental condition—is 6 months or more, almost to the day. Though inherently more severe, having a gun pointed at you once is less likely to be as devastating as being taken hostage for an extended period even if its without any physical injury.

Believing ourselves great at something that we excel at does not create much disturbance, for there is little discrepancy between what we conceive and reality. Taking ourselves to be less and actually being more leaves us pleasantly surprised frequently. Believing ourselves less and not performing well upholds a certain homeostasis. But, the extreme mismatch of holding ourselves special, though actually being quite ordinary or sub-par, is the fail-safe recipe for vindictive rage.

⑮ PERFECTIONISM IS IMPERFECT:
THE DRIVE TO DICHOTOMIZE

Perfectionists are romantics and idealists masquerading as pragmatists. Ironically, their obstinate demand for correctness leads unfailingly to failure, yet still they perpetually place blame on others, rather than realizing and revising the flaws in their own approach. They long to "teach people lessons." They are born optimists, awaiting human nature's overnight metamorphosis . . . which of course, never comes (and odds are, never will).

Instead, only their self-righteousness and bitterness grow, and at some juncture, try as hard as we (on the receiving end of the appraisal) might, we are all found guilty as charged: of the crime of being human.

Perfectionists are beset and (mis-)guided by the need to dichotomize the world into black-and-white, all-or-nothing oversimplifications. The allure of these oversimplifications is that they:

1. Feel good because they are uncomplicated and predictable, giving the world a sense of order and fairness (e.g., "You're either with us or against us"; "He asked for it").
2. Require less effort in the short term, as evaluations need only be made once, not on an individuated and ongoing basis. The downfall is that this "easier" ploy is frequently more costly in the end, a shortcut that ultimately leads to a dead end.

Among the perils are that zero-sum (i.e., all-or-nothing, win/lose) equations stimulate:

1. ARGUMENT: Debate is induced, as these judgments don't account for the exceptions to the rule.
2. FRUSTRATION: Because reality is not accurately reflected, expectations are foiled.
3. HELPLESSNESS: Multiple options and real choice are swapped for either–or/"do-or-die" ultimatum outcomes.
4. HYPOCRISY: Extreme standards are put in place that no one can maintain, *including* the person espousing them!

If we do not learn to live with the imperfections of others, we sentence ourselves to a hell of our own making, for we are not living in the world that we've been given.

Antidote

By utilizing a "we/us" framework in place of "me-against-you" exchanges, gaps in aspiration and understanding are lessened, rather than deepened.

"Some," but not all, is often the proper sum (e.g., when facing intractability such as, "What more do you want from me? I'm doing *all* I can," the response that's most likely being sought is: *some*thing).

Rather than evaluating people with generalities such as good or bad, better that we talk precisely of what exactly the disturbance is (sadistic, predatory, insensitive) or, even better yet, what the desired performance might be (empathic, restrained, thoughtful).

Possible pitfall: A favorite loophole used by character-disordered people—that is, those with chronically unhealthy patterns of interaction that disrupt almost every area of their life (social, romantic, familial, professional)—is to gauge without gradation, so that their abstinence from doing something is then inverted by them to equal having then actually done the contrary in its place. For example, such individuals might rationalize: "(Since I wasn't *quite* acting like an outright bitch), I was 'being nice'" via these inelegant determinations.

⑯ EXCESS OF RULES

Rules and laws are established when people do not trust that others will do what they "should." The more laws a society has, the less trust exists between its members.

Violent individuals do not become violent because of a lack of rules (i.e., anarchy), as is commonly held, but instead usually due to an excess of rules that construct a dynamic where choice is inhumanely limited.

a) Absolustic Thinking

By describing the world in too extreme and judgmental a fashion, depressed and/or aggressive individuals are left in feeble, optionless inner states where positive resolution is not possible. Black/white thinkers struggle to categorize and describe the entire chromatic range of life experiences with a vocabulary of, for all intents and purposes, only two words (i.e., good/bad, right/wrong, with/against, us/them).

These perfectionistic individuals are in recurrent states of mourning the loss of their perfectionistic ideals: the way things "should/should've" been. This basic "splitting" framework (i.e., divisive, polarizing conclusions) is founded on three key words:

Can't/couldn't: If I *can't* do anything else but this undesired course of action, then I am in a dependent state *without options*, and there is nothing to *think* about because right and wrong are predetermined in a *past-oriented* way. In reality, "I can't" translates more accurately into, "It's difficult, though there are options."

Had/have: If I really *have* to do what I am doing, then I am not responsible for the consequences at all. Thus, self-righteousness is fueled and others must be to blame (i.e., the principal origin of the verbal "You"-bait). "I have to" more reasonably translates into, "The other choices that are available are not acceptable or desirable to me."

Should/shouldn't: This obsession with doctrines assigns duties to others as well, and these perfectionistic expectations guarantee disappointment, because *even when someone does* what he or she "should" do, *it still isn't enough*. "You should" really translates into, "In my estimation, it seems that doing _____ might be better and more advisable."

Note: Most suicide notes are littered with liberal use of the above duties and obligations.

Antidote

When care is taken to enhance the accuracy of our statements through measured and balanced speech, pressure is relieved for both the sender and receiver of the message.

Some of the other most suspect absolustic words to look out for include:

- *forever/always/never*
- *best/worst*
- *all/every/none*
- *most/least/just*

Step one with many misguided interventions is the ideation, "I *have* to do something," which when distilled down to its essence equals the need to take action *even* when and if it is garnering the exact opposite outcome that was intended (i.e., persisting instead of electing to yield, pause, or retreat).

Words that positively supplant or alter the aforementioned absolutes include: *some, may/might, seems, a/an/one* (in place of *the*), *can/could* (countering *can't*), *probably* (modifying *should* and *would*), *almost* (which helps amend *always*).

The word *might* is especially mighty. It is non-alienating in that it allows for the recognition and coexistence of all possibilities.

b) Unacceptance

All individuals have the potential for violence. It is not the presence of an impulse that is the dilemma, it is the inability to control it—and, if the resulting action is severe enough, even one momentary lapse can be catastrophic (as we've already touched on previously).

Who among us is not a vengeful, perverted, suicidal, mass murderer in our heads? (. . . at least to *some* degree)?

If we do take aggressive action at all (which, fortunately, is a very rare occurrence), each and every one of us becomes violent at the exact same point: when something or someone has become intolerably unacceptable to us.

For most "normal" individuals that point comes very rarely, if at all, but it is invariably based around this feature of intolerability. For example, it is understandably intolerable to most people that anyone try to hurt them, someone they love, or another who is vulnerable, and at that point *most* of even the most peaceful people among us will become violent. In fact, many prosocial individuals are much more inclined to fight passionately in defense of others than *themselves*.

It follows that the more rules we have about the way things "should" be, the more frustration or disappointment we are likely to experience, and the more frequently we'll encounter circumstances that are unacceptable to us (e.g., "I *can't* take it anymore. I've had it!").

When people feel that something is unacceptable enough, they may even conclude that they have been granted license for capital punishment, acting as police, judge, jury, and executioner for even minor offenses—for example, the tragically oh-so-common occurrence of someone being shot for looking at another the "wrong way" or for cutting them off while driving (i.e., "road rage").

Antidote

People are almost always injured by individuals and in situations that they did not expect to be injured by or in. Otherwise, they usually would not have been in the situation to begin with or would've done what they could to prevent its outcome. (It is worth noting is that it is often "posers" who can prove the most dangerous, since it is they who tend to be inclined to do something drastic to try to prove that they are not one.)

Feeling safe does not equal being safe. Counterintuitively, safety comes most often from the recognition of danger. Acceptance of relative safety—at best—and of the potential for danger from anyone (including ourselves) better equips us to guard from it.

If we place others in the role of educator (via questions), we award ourselves greater occasions to be enlightened while concurrently being less threatening to them. Furthermore, it is usually much better that a seeming "rival" underestimate us than that we do so of him or her.

No matter how much we may know, we are incapable of knowing *every*thing (i.e., regardless how frequent the reminders that we aren't omnipotent—which is the also-troubling flipside of helplessness—they can almost never reach a point of omniscience). And no matter how "stupid" others may be, they know things that we do not, and therefore, we can learn from them. But only if we have interest and allow that learning to occur.

⑰ ANTIQUATED RELATIONAL CONCEPTS

To a large degree, most people behave in whatever way they are expected to behave. And most of us see what we expect to see, more than what is actually there.

"Seek and ye shall find," almost without fail.

Hopefully our guidance leads us towards that which is positive and away from negatives that often masquerade as inevitable (i.e., the past orientation of "the way things *are*").

a) "Enemy" Is the Enemy

The word *enemy* should long ago have been outmoded, relegated to the dustbins of history, as archaic as any Olde English. It has outlived its usefulness, but lingers systematically, the vernacular equivalent of an appendix.

The word *adversary* is more accurate.

We are infrequently, if ever, 100% right; and the other, regardless of just how off, has probably yet to quite reach 100% wrongfulness. Though there inevitably will be occasions of mutual discord, they are almost always potentially resolvable.

Enemy suggests a permanence to what are eventually transitory conflicts. Do we label the British, Native Americans, Mexicans, Germans, Japanese, etc., "enemies" today as we did so fervently before?

Should we have ever?

(In fact, are not many of our former enemies, today our greatest allies, and vice versa?)

Antidote

Viewing war, fighting, and conflict as inevitable not only increases the likelihood that they will occur, but actually ensures that at some point they will. If in place of the stance "I can't back down" as a tenant of manhood, "Fighting is not acceptable" was engendered, a gradual revolution of cooperation could be garnered.

Maybe, more than "being a 'man,'" be *human*.

Instead of just loving our country, love our world.

Some other obsolete, but persistent and pernicious phrases:

"You *have* to look out for 'Number One.'"

"Get them before they get you."

"*Just* do it."

"Take it *or* leave it."

"*Win* the war." (When usually, at best, a tentative truce can be forced.)

"Show *no* mercy. Take *no* prisoners."

"This must be done at *any* cost. *Or* else."

"*Never* surrender."

"You're *either* with us *or* against us."

"I'm *not* afraid of *any*body."

"They *deserved* it."

b) Compulsive Competitiveness

Unfortunately, one of the most prevalent philosophies espoused by Americans today is based on a falsehood.

"It's a dog-eat-dog world."

This statement is a factual inaccuracy since dogs *don't* eat dogs and, furthermore, they abide by a stringent set of social mores that promote alliance and coexistence. *Intraspecific slaughter* is almost exclusively a human anomaly.

Dogs might bite dogs; they might even kill each other in fantastically peculiar "natural-world" cases, but cannibalization is not part of their makeup. There are very few animals at all that do not obey one of the most essential elements for survival: an underlying and overriding need for cooperation.

More than "survival of the fittest," it really more closely resembles "attrition of the weakest," an evolutionary strategy that results in genetic elevation. If the strongest always fought faithfully to the death, the genetic outcome would, instead, be a backslide.

Antidote

Competition is based on the principle that for one to benefit, another must suffer. This position understandably promotes a paranoid mindset. If it is taken to be true that someone *has* to lose, certainly it makes perfect sense *then* to make well sure it isn't me.

Stressing a win–win outcome has a different objective: that of mutual benefit and gain versus the lopsided "winner takes all." The concept that someone has to be persecuted—to have or to have *not*—in order for another to prosper compounds the tendency towards offense ("strike first"), in place of more balanced, inoffensive strategies. Win–win structures allow for a broader range of positive, versus polarized and reactive, behavioral niches.

The drawback with even seemingly reasonable statements like "I don't have to win every battle" is that they entirely miss the crucial detail that we are rarely ever actually at war to begin with.

Interestingly, Japan and America share the same phrase, "Be sure to watch your back," but with very different meanings. Unlike the wariness it fosters in America, in Japan the message is one of vigilance to be sure that *you* are not inconveniencing others by blocking their way.

If the net effect of any relationship—whether short- or long-term—is win/lose, then it is inevitable that one of the two parties will be or is being exploited as a result.

Relentless competition consumes energy that could otherwise be used constructively and allow for frameworks where "many hands *can* make light work," indeed.

⑱ EXTREMES ARE *EXTREMELY* IMPORTANT

Extremes of any sort are unsettling because they almost always lead to imbalances. Wherever there is a disturbance of any kind, extremes of some sort are usually found. And it's not just someone who is too mean who may be the problem, but also someone who is *overly* nice. If it's "too good to be true," it probably really isn't true.

Extremes in any category deny complexity and seldom reflect the full reality of any situation. With their existence, generally a counterbalancing, phantom energy builds up that eventually explodes in a delayed and warped manner—like a slingshot being hurled after the tension is released—any time the overall stress load becomes too massive.

When encountering duress, most of us have the tendency to go to extremes by over- or underreacting, with either usually contributing to making bad situations worse—potentially turning what may have only been a tepidly troublesome situation into a full-blown crisis. (Anytime the middle goes missing—as in fascist regimes where too vast a void is created between rich and poor—the lust for revolution surfaces obediently like a corrective reflex.)

A large number of the worst accidents and injuries occur *during* accidents. In other words, the attempt to avert a fender bender collision entirely (i.e., perfectionistically) may lead to overcorrecting, turning too abruptly, flipping the car over, and much worse response. That is why sometimes the best advice in emergency situations is to do nothing or as little as possible until things can be better assessed and/or help arrives. (The same thing can happen in relationships, when someone hastily "jumps from the frying pan into the fire," leaving an unequivocally bad situation for one that ends up being fully disastrous.)

We have a profound built-in ability to sense the grace when what is being done is just enough (i.e., "not too little, not too much, but just right"). Even household pets have been shown to be aware of and influenced by equity (e.g., they will cease playing games that produce unfair, though otherwise beneficial, rewards). Our gut is rarely wrong in its sense that something is "off." Neglecting to identify precisely what is the disturbance (or that there is one at all) is where we most often go astray.

Especially potent is when two extremes merge and form a noxious fusion, whether it be two die-hard political parties wanting the same thing (but for different, though, equally unwholesome reasons) or the fact that the greatest exposure to assault occurs just on the fringe of busy areas (e.g., on a secluded side street off of a popular nightlife strip versus smack dab in the midst of the madness or in an utterly remote area where it is highly likely that there *is* "no one around" including would-be assailants).

a) Overperformance and Underperfomance

Relationships are hardly ever 50/50. Generally one party is carrying more of the emotional labor than the other. As humans, we tend to do only what we are required to do (the law of energy conservation) and thereby we can easily be trained into dependency and laziness. The less we are doing, the less we tend to be willing to do. And the longer that we don't do anything, the more that unequal effort becomes normalized as a precedent, which is encapsulated in the common refrain, "We've *always* done it this way."

Ultimately, the overperforming individual, no matter how great his or her drive and stamina, will become exhausted and withdraw. And when that person does *stop*, it will not be a subtle lessening of effort, but an extreme one—a "crash," metaphorically.

Since the world endlessly seeks equilibrium, at the very moment of that change, the underperforming individual will, almost without fail, suddenly spring into action, inverting this perfect asymmetry (by trying to make up for lost time and doing now what they probably should've been doing long before), which then only helps perpetuate the cycle of imbalance. Instead of sharing responsibility equally, one partner ends up chronically overextended and with their energies exploited, whether by either's design or not.

Antidote

Our strengths can work against us if they're used to garble or delay the consequences of reality. Overperformance cannot continue indefinitely and, eventually, the false foundation and fragile balance of the relationship(s) will collapse.

A key offset is admitting our own limitations while nurturing the strength of others. Ethical living is not as uncomplicated as doing the right thing. It requires additionally that we do these right things, within context, at the right times, and with the "right" people—that is, with those who are participating and have earned our efforts, versus the displacement of our love or wrath onto surrogates.

Frequently, explosive behavior emanates from a well-intended starting point: The desire to be "nice" or at least "not be 'mean' " leads many people to shy away from conflict. By not telling the truth about how one feels, the resentment is allowed to build until it is only expressed after it has inflated to toxic levels. This martyr behavior is, at its essence, dishonest and can result in all-or-nothing nonsense—like someone not wanting to hurt another's feelings now, but potentially being willing to "kick his ass" later.

Worse yet, the favored form of communication for many self-centered individuals is ESP—the expectation that we *should* already know what they think/need/want without their saying anything (or, at most, very little) at all. Customarily, that means that we're already in trouble—with a mark against us—before we've even really begun.

b) Active versus Subtle

Extremes act like a see-saw, with the more obvious extreme shadowed by its twin and more discreet pole. Often, the subtler, less active extreme is over-looked or dismissed. Though the dangers of the sub-tler extreme may develop in a slow-motion fashion, their eventual emancipation can be equally or even more harmful than their more noticeably disturbing counterparts (largely because the subtler ones seem to come out of nowhere).

Constant change is a byproduct of our quest for homeostasis. Reflecting this, the tendency of most aggressive adolescents is to mellow with time, while the challenge for the wallflower, the compulsive pla-cator, is to avoid abruptly attempting to make up for lost time indiscriminately and become a "rage-aholic," with no brakes from midlife on.

Interpersonally, seductions often comes as an onslaught (e.g., a "love bomb"). Though understand-ably these premature histrionics have their charm, the truth remains that "the higher we rise, the further we fall." Someone hating you on sight is understand-ably more alarming than someone who loves you instantaneously, but the latter can be just as lethal. That idealization contained in instant love can only be followed, at some juncture down the line, by the realization that we are not as wonderful (nor is any-body) as we may have first appeared. Plus, in many ways, someone "coming on too strong" can be a sign of an overall regulation problem (i.e., an instability in the arena of self control), and just like his or her ardor was unrestrained, so too might possibly be the fury that follows.

A person who boasts outright is clearly grandiose. But overly self-derogatory statements, such as "I *am* the worst singer ever," veil a subterranean grandios-ity. The truth is that the majority of us are most likely neither the best nor the worst, but simply mediocre. (Proclamations such as "I know the *best* hairdresser in the world" are delusion-by-proxy, borrowing their pretension from afar and indirectly, and acting all-too-revealing as to what the person fears most: being average).

Antidote

Any extreme is advisedly best viewed with wonder and consideration—and not just the person who doesn't seem to "give a shit about *any*one," but also the one who cares "*too* much"; not just the loud character, but also one who is unusually quiet.

The two fundamental things that we are advised to look for most closely—extremes and changes (of *any* kind)—are echoed by the fact that the two groups that are hardest to assess reside at the extremes—those whom we do not know, as well as those whom we "know" *too* well, and, consequently, often stop assessing at all (or as carefully).

The conscious hunt for recognizing changes in behavior (enhancing our inherent tendency to register any and all changes as prospective threats) requires that we are familiar with people's "baseline" behaviors—that is, their everyday, more-or-less routine ways of moving through the world. The fact is that most people's "neutral" is not really neutral; it is shaded by residual or core emotions that usually hint at their basic disposition (e.g., someone with a perpetual frown).

Embracing prevention of undesired outcomes as possible and valuable demands that we not only *don't* deny their warning signs, but that we actually search for them avidly, considering not just methods (i.e., what someone is doing or how something is being done), but also ends (i.e., what they result in). As an anti-example, there are some people who approach life as a checklist to be dutifully completed, following which just rewards are assumed to be all but short of guaranteed (e.g., "If I am generous at work, people should be nice to me"), but then fail to adapt to the intricate and changing reality around them and only recognize that something is amiss too late (e.g., not noticing that their child or spouse is miserable until after they've already left and the rift is nearly unfixable).

Sadly, most tragedies are preceded by *ever* closer close calls that went haplessly unheeded (e.g., the anorexic who disregarded multiple fainting spells leading up to a full-blown seizure).

⑲ UNBOUNDED BOUNDARIES

Where there is a disturbance of any sort, usually a boundary issue is at play, whether it is someone who is standing too close to us in line at the bank or a person who lives entirely shut off from most direct contact with society.

a) Transactional

Violence results from chronically bad boundaries or from an abrupt infringement of exiting boundaries.

If boundaries are too rigid (e.g., refusing to listen), little communication can occur. If boundaries are *too* loose and permeable, it is like living without an immune-system; proper interpersonal maintenance cannot occur via suitable self defense (i.e., prompt recognition of another's far out-of-line inappropriateness), *every*one is given the "benefit of the doubt," and it is assumed that it is I, not they, who is somehow in the wrong (for example, anyone who makes sudden, uninvited physical contact with us).

Note: most extraordinary behavior is not random; it usually occurs in clusters. Not only is someone more likely to die behind the wheel of a car when not wearing a seatbelt, but, furthermore, people who don't wear seatbelts are more likely statistically to drive recklessly in the first place. Some actions are so abnormal (i.e., the majority of people *never* do them, even once)—like murder, rape or any calculated exploitation of others—that they are more revelatory (i.e., that there is a profound unwellness in that person's moral integrity) versus simply being demonstrative (i.e., that they, too, like us all are simply "human"). Therefore, the more peculiar the factor, the more likely it is to act as an indicator of deeper plights.

Generally, the further out of proportion a person's reaction is to us (i.e., when the punishment doesn't fit the crime), the more likely that there is a prehistory to which we are not privy (e.g., for years many *other* people have also thrown their cigarette butts outside that person's apartment window, so it is already one of his or her pet peeves, and thus why the person is so instantly aroused by it).

Antidote

What we can strive for is *complementarity* by inter-
acting with each individual before us on a case by
case basis, not only varying our approach with every
individual, but *even with the same individual*, who
will not be entirely consistent in his or her behavior
all of the time.

Such mental suppleness runs counter to the tendencies of violent individuals who use a "one-size-
fits-all" approach, in a world that demands far more
sophistication, versatility, and sensitivity.

b) Internal

Those who lack internal organization and stability subsist without a navigational system. As a result, these individuals are seized by whatever emotion or impulse is strongest at any given moment, which in turn is usually determined by chance encounters with the world.

If we do not keep a division between thought and feeling (or distinct feelings themselves), a destructive synergy can be formed through which all strong emotions are fused into one uncontrollable whole (e.g., the male who might feel that the only strong emotion that it is acceptable for him to express is anger, and which therefore acts as a stand-in for any and all of his passion).

Additionally, if the split between thoughts and feelings is too austere, our decision making and perceptual skills will be deeply compromised from the lack of integration between heart and mind (i.e., "the left hand not knowing what the right is doing"). Note: the split named by schizophrenia is not in the personality, as is often inaccurately claimed, but instead between thought and emotion with that disconnection instigating the most severe psychoses.

Antidote

Recognition that we simply cannot do *every*thing we feel like doing is, paradoxically, the ultimate freedom (i.e., of choice), as opposed to the superficial, infantile freedom of "doing it all" (which rejects choice entirely).

It can be crucial to verify that when we speak about what we "feel," we are actually talking about emotions.

Most people deceive themselves and others through the use of "I-feel-*thought*" versus "I-feel-*emotion*" statements. The word *like* is a dead giveaway of such derailments. For example, "I feel *like* that is *wrong*"—which, in actuality, is rendering a judgment, not a feeling. "I feel *angry*," in contrast, is a clear-cut statement of the person's emotion at that time (i.e., anger).

c) Temporal

Trouble with boundaries exists not just between parties, but also in relationship to time.

If past conflicts have not been properly processed or maintained, they leach into future frustrations. Taken to an extreme, nearly all interactions become crisis-laden when overcome by a flood of welled-up and swollen resentments (e.g., the cliché of the person snapping at the dinner table because someone is slurping his or her soup too loudly or another being willing to batter a stranger over a parking space).

Antidote

Keeping our focus in the here-and-now, and *not* dragging past-oriented baggage into the fray as additional weight, contributes constructively to solutions rather than destructively to blame.

Use of "subordinate clauses of time" (e.g., the words *after*, *now*, *once*, *since*, or *then*) and "sequential" terms (e.g., *first*, *next*, *another*) explicitly refer to progress, and are all founded on the presupposition that a mutual goal is *already* in process and is achievable. For example, the statement "*After* we finish the interview, *then* the *next* thing we can do is call and find out what other appointments might be available."

The words *permanence* and *constancy* are used in psychological circles to refer to the ability to imagine something's existence beyond our own. The classic example is a development one: A very young child will be distressed if we move a cookie behind, say, the cupboard, and he would believe that it no longer exists. At a certain age, however, most young children realize that the cookie isn't really gone—it's just hidden for the moment.

Adults with serious emotional problems may be impoverished in this area and therefore easily led astray by whatever and whomever is immediately before them. Due to this world of ever-changing parts and players, they exhibit greater volatility (e.g., fidelity is next to impossible unless the partner is eternally present, as in their absence the partner and the bond to them become, in essence, less real).

Relating to a person or event as an all-or-nothing/on–off experience does not allow us to combine conflicting elements. Without this tolerance for mingling, contamination is construed to occur anytime any variety or deviation is revealed—what was good becomes suddenly bad. This "formula" guarantees that no union will be lasting, as flaws will be revealed in everything/anybody sooner or later, and those flaws will then cannibalize the positives.

Often we see adolescents with stereotypically tortured countenances accompanied by family in public settings as they struggle through the throes of a later stage of this process—which entails not only the discovery that their parents are not perfect, but also, the undeniable recognition that the child still needs and loves (. . . and, even worse yet, probably is *a lot* like) "them." Maturity is fostered through our ability to tolerate ambivalence, integrate good and bad feelings into one entirety, and, thereby, form more sophisticated and intricate definitions.

Antidote

People can most precisely be described as verbs/adverbs, not nouns/adjectives. For example, "She *is being difficult*" is more accurate than "She *is difficult*." The first describes behavior in action, whereas the second proclaims an unchanging state of being. Similarly, "What *he did was stupid*" is preferable to "He *is stupid*." Describing behavior, rather than ascribing labels (i.e., globalizing), helps build objectivity and tolerance.

Even the smartest and most "perfect" among us sometimes say and do stupid or bad things—with alarming frequency, if strictly analyzed. But very few of us consider ourselves "stupid" or "bad" as a result. And, in most cases, we are (*mostly*) right.

By conditioning ourselves to craft descriptions as specifically and accurately as possible, and to celebrate life's inevitable follies and differences, we can inoculate ourselves from some of their impact. The stop-gag maneuver is to vigil that we are not condemning others wholesale (e.g., "That guy's an idiot. I hate people like that."), but instead concentrate on only the single instance in question (e.g., "Cutting someone off like that in traffic can be a really dangerous thing to do").

㉟ CULTURAL INERTIA

Three primary obstacles serve as impediments to growth and progress in individuals and groups:

- Opting for the short-term versus long-term
- Focusing on probability over possibility
- Mistaking false-positives for truth

a) Opting for the Short-Term versus Long-Term

What regularly is not incorporated into evaluations of what is advisable behavior is whether or not the given strategy is sustainable.

In the short term, my hitting the wall or yelling at others may seem to reduce stress, but in the long term, the net effect is that I am subjected to more pressure (e.g., being fired because of my behavior).

In the short term, if I ignore a problem I may, in fact, dodge confrontation, but in the long run an even more sizable showdown awaits.

The bottom line for all short-term "thinkers" is the unavoidable, but denied reality of "Pay me now or pay me later."

Whatever we strive to avoid entirely, by taking the "short-cut," has simply been postponed and will eventually have to be paid back down the line with interest and come-uppance.

Antidote

When evaluating options in any situation of importance, it is advisable to include an exploration of long- and long*er*-term consequences. Doing so can thwart our myopia and protect us from delayed, boomeranging, or counterbalancing corrections that that often sneak up on us.

Note: On the whole, predation's strategy—which we are largely guided by—is a lazy one: do nothing most of the time (e.g., bask in the sun), then do a whole lot all at once at another's life-or-death expense (i.e., prey on them).

b) Focusing on Probability over Possibility

In making predictions, most people fall short generally because they focus exclusively on what they perceive to be the most probable outcome—even though, worse yet, they are often mistaken to begin with in their guesses as to what is most likely.

No matter how liable something is, or is not, to occur, there almost always remains the *possibility* of it being contradicted.

A teenage male *is* much more likely to engage in dangerous behavior than a middle-aged female, but that does not eliminate the *possibility* that a given middle-aged female may be the exception and act out in extremely negative ways (e.g., a seasoned middle-school teacher going ballistic in the face of a large 14-year-old boy who somehow miraculously manages to maintain his composure).

Antidote

Predictions ideally include at least a cursory 360-degree survey of *all* options and possibilities. By "entertaining the absurd" (i.e., ruling out nothing, *in theory*), we reduce the chances that we will underestimate situations, overlook the more subdued extremes that are looming, or miss the less obvious solutions that are available.

A willingness to reflect on even the most extreme alternatives can make less dramatic ones suddenly appear not so unreasonable and possibly even suitable after all.

A skeletal example of the failure to search beyond surfaces is this: In medical settings, as well as with children and animals, what often is misguidedly leapt to first are commentaries on the individual's character rather than identifying any of the possible underlying physical causes (e.g., being sick, tired, hungry, too hot/cold) that account for so many of the taxing behaviors that arise with these populations and in these environments. Typically, the lower the cognitive ability (e.g., someone who is nonverbal, drunk, or demented), the greater the likelihood that there is an unmet physical cause at play.

A general guideline is to "ignore the behavior but not the individual."

And a grand goal is for our foresight to become less clouded and more closely aligned with the accuracy of hindsight.

Possible pitfall: Incessantly frustrated individuals have a tendency to confuse what *can* be with what "is," by inverting what's possible and what's probable. The inability to accept imperfection leads to a cross-contamination backwash from exceptional events (i.e., an isolated error leads to a permanent, usually irreversible conclusion). The draw of these negative expectations is that the prognosticator will almost always be proven "right" *eventually*, some of the time, even if its only 1 in a trillion. Theirs is a conservative and pessimistic model, acting as "I told you so" claim-stakers for calamity.

c) Mistaking False-Positives for Truth

Experience does not always strengthen our ability in any specific area. In fact, it can often even work against us, placing us "in a rut" where inquisitiveness and innovation are stifled. The longer that one has done something a certain way, the more resistant he or she is likely to be to the unlearning (and admittance of his or her own imperfection) that any incorporation of a new method requires.

Also, the more times or the longer that I engage in a certain behavior without negative consequences, the more likely I am to underestimate its dangers *and* overestimate my personal powers—that is, I start to believe in my "individual invincibility." Bad habits can easily develop under the auspices of doing what "has always worked" or what you're "supposed to."

If a given strategy *never* worked, people would eventually stop using it at all. But virtually any tactic will work *some* of the time. By focusing selectively only on when a particular strategy is or isn't effective, subjectivity is fed—which increases the room for error.

These false positives thrive amidst the fertile ground of past orientation that forms so much of our strife. As noted earlier, think of how often we hear the defense, "But we've always done it like this" to support the continuation of an approach, despite its proven ineffectiveness. The tragicomic truism is that most conflict is resolved not because of how, but *in spite* of, the way we "handled it."

Antidote

To compensate for our natural "repetition compulsion"—that which we have already done, we are most likely to do again—it is advantageous to challenge the foreseeable past-oriented, historical resistance (e.g., "That's just not the kind of person I am") by reserving a sensible degree of doubt as ballast.

We have an almost moral obligation to provide others with accurate and honest feedback related to their conduct, lest harmful behaviors recur or even proliferate by way of our implied tolerance. Ignoring a pending problem is simply the sly, passive duality of creating it in the first place.

"Okay, but what if (we tried)_____" is ground-zero for healthy inquisitiveness and invention.

(21) THE VIOLENCE OF COMPARISONS

A most common but subtle form of abuse is comparison. Comparison superimposes a win–lose/more-less framework and promotes limitations to achievement that do not intrinsically exist. It often acts as the low-grade, entry-level gateway to greater insult.

As a result of an inability to individuate (i.e., due to the combination of poorly-constructed boundaries and a lack of specificity), overly concrete thinkers are often severely limited in their capacity to see any one thing independently. Hand-in-hand with past orientation, they are compelled then to relate almost every experience to another that they've already had (e.g., "This is *exactly* the same as _____," which, of course, only sharpens the well-trodden path of past orientation).

Modern life has become an increasingly referential, house of mirrors of comparisons in which everyday life is frequently described as being "just like that scene from _____" (from which can be inferred that reality can never be quite as good).

a) Differences as Inequality

That someone is taller than us does not alter our own height. *Other than* does not necessarily have to equal *less than*. The contrast has simply altered perception, as well as shunned deeper investigation of the pros and cons of any single feature. For example, a larger car may truly be safer structurally, but it also, as a result of its size, is more likely to be hit by and/or hit something.

One of the most widespread comparisons is made to precedents (i.e., past orientation, yet again), as if whatever was done before is irrevocably valid and the status quo should undoubtedly be upheld (if this were true, than slavery, human sacrifice, and countless other barbaric actions would still be valid institutional practices).

An even worse use of comparative thinking is in the defense of negative activities by relating them to something even worse (e.g., "Maybe I do drink a little more than I should, but at least I'm not a junkie"; "Just be glad I'm even doing *this* much"; and the ever-popular, It's not like I killed someone").

Antidote

Discussions of contrasting value are better discouraged in place of searching for diverse merit.

Learning to recognize and value different levels of achievement, as opposed to the more pervasive mentality of "every man for himself," generates an enhanced abundance for all.

One can almost imagine the monumental difference, if stadiums full of children were instead chanting, "We're Number *N*-one! We're Number *N*-one!"

Celebrating that we are not static, but fluid, living, complex beings promotes devotion to many levels of performance and not just overt achievement. We are all works in progress. Many of us live our lives as though we are constantly at the end or beginning of our story, when in fact we are most likely somewhere in the middle. Indeed, most great successes are preceded by decisive "failure" of some sort. It is at our own peril that we arrogantly rest on our laurels or dismiss others as entirely predestined and predictable—particularly the "late bloomers" in both good and ill behaviors. (For example, the fact that someone was an outstanding employee for decades matters little if later they crack and go on a murderous rampage at work.)

It is not enough to "do" the right thing, unless we are able to *keep* doing it. Ownership (i.e. acquiring something) is more glamorous and attractive than the hum-drum, day-to-day toil of maintenance. But it is through maintenance that consistency and commitment are proven.

Tributes are strongest when they stand independently—for example, "You are beautiful" versus "You are the most beautiful person I've ever met." Those draped in superlatives come tainted by the undertow that someday they, too, will be usurped, diminished, or annihilated by the implicit rivalry they are built upon.

Possible pitfall: Differentiation is a natural consequence of any group setting. The easiest method for getting a need met is not outright competition but, instead, through an exploitation of unoccupied social niches. Theories about the dynamics of birth order in families are based on these tendencies. We can correctly expect that we will find similar stratifications throughout history, including the present, and across all classes, cultures, and age groups, and that contrarians will inevitably abound no matter how strong any one cause or idea. Due to this, the more harshly we oppose someone, often the more differentiated and radicalized they will become as a defense.

b) Essentialization: Unconditional Hate

No matter where it takes place in the world, when we examine fanatical acts of violence such as genocide, they all share one founding pretense: that of essentialization.

Essentializations universally identify the other as subhuman—for example, *rat*, *snake*, *parasite*, *cancer*, *cockroach*—yet consist of the unlikely combination that the vilified is "pathetic," but still somehow simultaneously dangerous. The end product: a lethal hybrid of two extremes.

It doesn't stop there. The persecuting group members essentialize themselves, also. Not very surprisingly, they place themselves at the other, lofty end whereby they are not only incomparably superior, but are actually "*the* chosen." Given the extremity of these positions, the rift between the two factions becomes almost unbridgeable, the tension intolerable, and coexistence is then no longer seen as feasible. We can find nearly innumerable historical events where two entrenched groups have created untenable, seemingly unfixable chasms of conflict between them.

Wherever bias is found, evaluations tend to have been made in a selective fashion—defining individuals or cultures by their best *or* worst qualities alone.

Manipulators must first manipulate themselves.

The ultimate self-perpetuation of these overly reduced, one-dimensional verdicts is assured by the inclusion of an automatic defense system, whereby judgments travel along a one-way circuit with no possible reversals or revisions. These networks diligently reject even the most miniscule deviation from the party line, branding any question or even the *slightest* doubt as a terrible menace as well as self-fulfilling "proof" as to why followers must cease having contact with any outsiders. With cults, this tactic of zero tolerance for doubt or questioning is a defining trait, and one of the more dangerous methods of mind control through which disbelief is no longer an allowable option at all.

This austerity reaches a crescendo when membership starts being denied to any who aren't devout *enough* so that even they risk ending up disqualified and excluded if certain arbitrary (i.e., highly subjective) standards are not met, as in, "He's 'Italian', but he's not *really* an Italian," or, "She's got the degree, but she's not really a *doctor* doctor."

The most vicious comparison is to superlatives, which as mentioned earlier, dooms everyone to eventual failure (e.g., "Yes, you are a man. You're just not man *enough*."; "He's smart, but not *quite* brilliant.").

Antidote

Only when we embrace complexity, doubt, and uncertainty can the possibility exist of exceptions that defy the rules. Assessments then can be approached as ongoing, evolving processes that require sustained effort (e.g., a classroom teacher attempting to view students as if for the first time each day, even though it may be the end of the school year).

Words have power. How we name things influences how we perceive them, and care is best taken how we do so. When we label whole groups in highly derogatory ways, we act irresponsibly and in a callous fashion. We are essentializing, and by doing so, we strip the situation of depth as well as our own contributions and responsibility. Taking greater care with how we frame and present our thoughts is a first step towards dismantling any inclination towards essentialization.

Often, *seem*[s], and *many* (but not *all*) are key words that help resist the descent into essentialization—and the unconditional hate it sponsors.

(22) SELECTIVE COMPASSION:
THE DISTURBINGLY-SIMILAR OTHER

Maximum animosity often arises not from what is most radically different but, counterintuitively, from that which is most alike, though *still* not *quite* precisely the same. Although the disparity is small, it is so near that it can become excruciating. Examples of disturbingly-similar others abound in families where two members quarrel incessantly because they are "too much alike." It may be that they, genetically speaking, are too close for comfort.

Most individuals can easily give compassion to a child or creature that is clearly disadvantaged or different from them. The truer challenge comes in tolerating another's struggles even when those struggles too faithfully parallel your own. For example, it can be extremely trying to witness the relapse of a friend who is an addict when we, too, are in recovery. It can also be difficult to genuinely support someone's success when it occurs in our chosen field (as opposed to in areas where we have no aspirations whatsoever), just as it can be a challenge to withstand verbal assaults that are nearly on target, and therefore infuriating, in contrast to those that are way, *way* off the mark and consequently only mildly irritating, at most (i.e., cases in which we might earnestly feel that we have "little left to prove").

Antidote

Loving someone who is distant and dependent comes more easily to many than loving someone who can equally provide or withhold it, and requires a more profound sharing of influence and vulnerability.

By willing ourselves to lend understanding where and when it is hardest, our capacity for lovingness expands, strengthening through use, like a muscle. There is not some finite amount available, as "the myth of scarcity" (i.e., that positive experiences and sensations come in chillingly limited quantities) would have us believe. The results of "practicing patience" rather than "getting angry" are diminished hostility and broadened awareness, for when we really need it. If I allow myself to be tested and frayed by the little things, then, fear deeply for me if something ever really, *truly* goes wrong (e.g., if someone pummels another over their having bumped into them by accident, what might they be capable of if they were ever fired from work, betrayed romantically, etc.?).

㉓ ISOLATION & HABITUAL AMBIVALENCE

How do people get to the point of committing heinous acts of violence? The answer is: gradually. Step-by-step they drift away from social norms until before they realize it, they are engulfed in a new, subterranean reality.

It is their own ambivalence that enables them to flirt and fantasize with an impulse, until it becomes more tangible and real. Revealingly, extreme *and* habitual ambivalence (versus *some* moderate ambivalence and doubt) is the one symptom that is shared clinically by virtually all mental health diagnoses, be they of personality, mood, or thought.

The "best of intentions" transform into the *worst* of intentions, in secrecy. The more isolated the individual becomes, the more his or her thoughts go untested by truth. As he or she becomes more preoccupied with inner fantasies and assumptions, the more a sense of normalcy and inevitability pervades their increasingly distorted perspective.

Most premeditatedly violent individuals trick themselves into a behavior by not fully committing to it until the last minute. The upside of this approach is that until these people actually take outright action, the possibility remains of convincing them otherwise. Many are the tales of premeditated violence, where assailants state that right up to the very moment of the crime, they *still* were not entirely certain whether they were going to follow through with what they had planned and prepared to do, in some cases for years.

Isolation can be psychological, not just physical. In fact, the disparity of being amidst a crowd but not actually recognized or understood can lead to an even more acute sense of separation.

Many privileged or powerful people become isolated when:

- They are surrounded only by "yes" people who are afraid to question them or tell the truth.
- They themselves feel that they must fulfill others' superhuman (perfect or superior) expectations of them, and therefore they cannot admit shortcomings or ask for help.

Judgmental environments act paradoxically as breeding grounds for all that which they endeavor to repress. If I cannot at the least admit what I feel, I certainly cannot ask for the help I may need in order to *not* act on these feelings. Thus, these actions becoming a reality or not is consigned to an all-or-nothing equation, with no balanced middle ground (e.g., verbal) in between to help relieve the strain.

Antidote

Our ability to adapt to almost anything ensures our survival in even the most unfavorable circumstances, short of those that physically kill us. The risk of this ability to acclimatize so well is that, after the initial painful and arduous transition, we can potentially become so desensitized to our new conditions that we grow unaware of how dramatically *we've* changed as a result.

Reassurance can be found in studies that have consistently indicated that good influences far outweigh the bad. Even one compensatory relationship, such as a mentor or relative who "sees" a child, can offset a world of hurt. It is the want entirely of any sort of salve or shelter, from which the most horrific doings arise (e.g., mass murder).

It can be helpful to remain mindful that thinking about doing something *is* still "doing something." It is the first step towards action. Almost all undesired behavior is preceded by two steps:

1. Preoccupation
2. Rehearsal/flirtation (i.e., acting without actually *yet* "taking action").

Monitoring where our thoughts drift can allow us to introduce substitutes (e.g., when we feel like smoking a cigarette, brushing our teeth instead) in place of missteps—so that we are guiding our thought processes rather than standing by passively while they are kidnapped. By doing this, we can potentially stop obsessive, life-of-their-own fantasies from developing further, and be better prepared—both *before* and in the heat of the moment—to elevate the "good" intentions of our unaroused self into concrete actions.

㉔ RELATIONSHIP QUICKSAND

Odds are, if we find ourselves asking atypically negative questions about another individual—"Is he psycho?"—the solemn answer is: yes.

The unconscious drive to replicate past traumas is a most perverse manifestation of our tendency towards repetition in all things. Thus, it its best that we are careful as to what and whom we expose ourselves. That which we start, we may not be able to finish . . . but it may finish us.

Almost anything can have an inherent addictive quality, leading us to repeat it. Repeating what we have already done not only provides at least some negligible margin of safety (i.e., as bad as it might be, it didn't kill us the first or other times, the way something newer might), but also, habit helps automate our behavior so that our consciousness is freed up for other, fresher pursuits.

Many are drawn towards hazards in a hope that re-experiencing a known jeopardy will lead to mastery via a different outcome or their being rescued this time. Sadly, neither of these usually occurs. Instead, the person's tendency towards victimization only becomes more deeply engrained (e.g., the despondent face of a battered individual can act like a magnet to abusive personalities).

Additionally, many people fear the void with which they might be left once conflict has ceased, since militarization or anguish may have become a central basis and organizational structure for their existence.

The two global red flags that a relationship is troubled are:

1. If we feel better (e.g., tremendous relief) when we are not with the person.
2. Whenever we find ourselves talking about someone to others in great disproportion to the value of the relationship.

Self-centered people have an incredible ability to make themselves the center of attention—whether positive or negative. They are often infamous, sometimes reaching almost mythological status, due to the efforts of countless people who have never even met them before, but nonetheless have invested massive effort to analyze their behavior on behalf of a loved one who is directly ensnared by them.

a) The Addictive Cycle: Giving the Right Answer for the Wrong Question

What draws people to, and keeps them in relationships with, chronically unhealthy people? Largely, it is because even the most polluting character has *some* appealing qualities, and it is these that motivate their partners to keep reinvesting their relational energies to them. In fact, with extreme individuals, the good qualities not only stand in dramatic distinction to the bad, but often are every bit as extraordinary as their capacity for ill. "The brighter the light, the darker the shadow," as they say.

The very fragments that cause these individuals to discard others (viewing partials—out-of-the-ordinary misconduct or errors of even the *slightest* degree as poisoning, zero-sum equations) are what drive others to reinvest in them (seeing these non-representative positive and appropriate behavioral exceptions as "glimmers of hope"). What would normally be a strength on the part of the victim (his or her own introspection and optimism) is exploited by the other in a parasitic way (e.g., "You *just* have to get to know him better. He's not *always* that way," in reference to the professional hit man).

Practiced manipulators have a distinct knack for inspiring in others the guilt and remorse that is devoid in them. That is, after they have placed us in awkward positions due to their grossly overstepping boundaries, we find often ourselves adrift in existential neverlands wondering, "Am *I* being selfish (or mean) for asking him to not smoke in the car?" or even worse, being sucked into conclusions like, "Maybe I'm the one with the problem. Maybe it's *me* who's crazy."

The trap is the cyclical, but false hope that a person who is behaving irrationally can be appealed to rationally, through reason.

"If I could just get her to understand, then she would finally get it—that I'm a good person" or "I know *this* time it'll be different."

The hunt for an "aha" moment of insight and enlightenment in the partner is the equivalent of a spiritual Ponzi scheme, and through it, the host allows the feasting to continue until he or she is depleted.

Repeated attempts to help an emotionally unwell person are like eating or exercising on their behalf, and then asking, "Don't you feel better now?" We are trying to do for them something that they can only do for themselves. They feel worse and grow more resentful, witnessing our efforts that are lacking in effect, and we grow bloated or fatigued due to having eaten or labored for two.

Past orientation and loss aversion—"I know this

is bad, but what'll come next may be even worse"—both rear their ugly heads when the fear of what may lurk just over the horizon keeps people settled in unsettling settings.

A telltale sign that someone is near rock bottom in a relationship is when the abuser reaches a point of criticizing and being irritated by the partner's most essential behaviors (e.g., the way they eat, sleep, talk, or even breathe).

A ruling paradox of domineering people is that the terror of abandonment is largely what drives them to be so controlling, but this behavior itself acts as the ultimate insurance that they will in time be abandoned by just about everyone.

Antidote

Recurrent behaviors are undeniable indicators of larger truths and patterns. Someone who crosses certain bright lines of proper conduct (e.g., deliberately scheming to humiliate someone; torturing animals), not just once—which is *already* exceptional—but many times, is perilously beyond repair.

And it is terribly important to duly note that it is not our job to fix anyone else anyway, in the first place.

We can up our interpersonal literacy by scrutinizing the cycle of highs and lows in our relationships to try to make sure that they have not become addictive (i.e., produced an adrenaline dependency), and that we are not substituting damaging drama for true, nurturing passion.

A good measure to implement is to spell out the advice you would give to another if he or she were in your present situation and then to take that exact same advice yourself, without excuses. Amazingly, people often allow themselves to be physically tormented and abused in their own home by a "loved one," yet if you ask them what they would do in reaction to the identical behavior from a stranger, they invariably are crystal clear and adamant that they would immediately resist or expel the danger (e.g., "Of course I would never let a violent drug addict into my home. What do you think I am, crazy?").

b) (Out of) Control Freaks

The hallmark of micro-managing "control freaks" is that their interest lies not with any outcome, in and of itself, but instead with their having been the one to have influenced the outcome, regardless of what it is. This subjective striving drives them to twist meaning into self-contradictory knots, whereby what may have been a mandate yesterday, easily becomes a dire and unforgivable error today if it was not they who directly determined the current course of action.

This inconsistency is disorienting to everyone in their sphere. The situation usually deteriorates until even the most obvious details are doubted, fear pervades, and the world is literally turned upside down, like left becoming right, only to be reversed again later . . . and then again.

Past-oriented individuals are not so much role-players as role-*givers and* scorekeepers, tallying up a litany of imagined wrongs.

Those who cannot control themselves attempt to control others, which, ironically, leads in due course to *their* being controlled externally (e.g., via prison, divorce, assault). They are terrified of their own dependency on others (since they lack genuine inner autonomy) and therefore habitually push others away unconsciously.

Antidote

Before entering into any venture with someone who has proven routinely erratic (i.e., a byproduct of subjective states of being), it is useful to have total clarity and establish clear contracts and guidelines. This preciseness compels the other to not only acquire some of the power that he or she so desperately seeks, but also the responsibility that he or she so compulsively denies.

By allowing someone to trespass on us emotionally or socially, we help contribute to poisonous behaviors that affect others (and society as a whole) as well implicitly verifying for the violating individual that his or her conduct is acceptable, necessary or, worst of all, noble.

Remaining lucid about the origins of the conflict is extremely important when dealing with those who have impaired boundaries. What is paramount is not who is to blame, but more precisely, who is responsible. The other person's problem need not become ours, particularly when it could've been prevented by him or her in the first place. True tragedies are rare; they are the outcomes that really weren't preventable and for which no one at all is wholly responsible (e.g., *actual* accidents versus regular, recurring patterns of behavior).

Generally, it is best to delay and see if overarching behavior self-resolves. If it does not, in some peculiar cases, it is most effective to then skip a step and intervene at the level that matches them (i.e., as if we had already made the previous intervention and it had proven ineffectual). Otherwise, we risk playing a game of catch-up with them due to their having mistaken our tolerance for timidity.

Possible pitfall: What is most difficult to adapt to is constant change. Though we have the ability to bend to most circumstances, it is the readjusting that is the most strenuous. The majority of traumas occur during intervals of change. That is why alcoholics are at their most acute risk during the first few days after they stop drinking, though in the long run it is better for them; why many with mental health conditions have episodes during or following traveling (which disrupts their routine); and also why most serious accidents occur at intersections or when someone has switched modality (immediately after shifting from walking to driving or driving to walking). Psychological terrorists use methods of "consistent inconsistency" to interrogate those in custody. Resistance is usually more quickly dissolved by alternating "good cop/bad cop" than through a steady, force-fed diet of abuse.

(25) THE THREE PRIMARY PSYCHOLOGICAL DEFENSE MECHANISMS:

DENIAL, PROJECTION, & REACTION FORMATION

Denial: If reality is not to one's liking, the most basic approach is to deny its existence entirely. For example, a person might scream, "I'm not angry!" even when the tension in his or her face, fists, and voice indicates otherwise. Empathy is nearly impossible to develop if we do not first know what we feel ourselves and, therefore, how what another person is feeling might be akin.

Projection: If a problem is no longer deniable, then customarily people begin to assign blame externally as a way to rid themselves of responsibility for what is indeed happening. This defensive stance accounts for the tragic phenomenon of "blaming the victim." Because the victim is frighteningly similar to us, we distance ourselves from the vulnerability of victimhood by finding fault with them. This tactic helps to restore our sense of control and safety, our belief that it—the crime or tragedy—*still* can't happen to us (the "right" people), *but only to them* (the "wrong" people). A crucial distinction is that when something is amiss, introspective people are inclined to ask what *they* are doing wrong, whereas problem-producing cohorts ask unfalteringly how they have *been wronged*.

Reaction formation: If a given emotion is unacceptable, then often its opposite is superimposed in an over-compensatory effort to mask and conceal the truth. Think of the amorous relations that are often preceded by intense hostility or how those that lack internal structure are so perpetually attracted to positions of authority (i.e., where *they* are "in charge"—e.g., police, managers, teachers). We see, too, the common hypocrisy of homophobia, which needs no elaboration beyond the headlines.

Like an unintentional Don Quixote, those who walk through the world broadcasting challenge postures (e.g., chest puffed out, nose in the air) make their fear transparent by way of this interpersonal arms race. A spouse innocently "liking" a coworker should usually be less cause for alarm than frequent protestations about someone "they can't stand," for why do they care so much? Frequently, that which repels someone—whatever they reject or disown—is a much more powerful indicator of what they will later become than that which they aspire to be. Be careful what you hate. (Even better yet, don't "hate" at all.)

Antidote

Staying open theoretically to *all* possibilities, as remote as some might seem, keeps us invested in solutions and progress. A willingness to listen (and regard all input and energy as sources of potentially usable instruction) sensitizes us to intricacies we may otherwise have missed and helps keep the focus on learning, not labeling.

Just as neurologists tell us that we can benefit from trying new activities and altering routines (e.g., brushing our teeth with the nondominant hand), considering new perspectives can act as yoga for the brain, stretching our neural "muscles" and helping us develop greater mental and emotional flexibility. Primary elements that block people from making these efforts towards deepening understanding are laziness (i.e., energy conservation) plus the fear of having to confess that perhaps their previous ideation about people and things was and is "wrong."

It is vital to recognize that within every negative statement is embedded its opposite: **"I'm not bothered by that"** is founded on **"I *am* bothered by that"**; **"I don't like him"** only exists due to **"I *do* like him."** It is to our advantage to explore these unintentional truths more deeply, rather than disregard them—both as the sender and receiver.

Possible pitfall: The heart of a negative message is the positive message that it negates. The foundation of "Don't yell" is the command "Yell," which its countermand cannot exist without. When we speak in negatives, we unwittingly give free advertising about the very thing we ostensibly are trying to abolish. Thereby we create a double bind (i.e., a "damned if you do/damned if you don't") in which the negative has to be done as a result of the negative character of the command. The direction "Don't think about ice cream" virtually guarantees that the listener will do precisely that: think about ice cream. In giving a negative instruction, one must first tell someone *what* to do in order for it then to become possible to immediately revoke the phrase and admonish him or her not to *do it*. (Note: mixed-message parenting has been found to be the single compellingly prevalent "nurture" feature of schizophrenics' backgrounds.)

DIPLOMATIC COMMUNICATION
and POTENTIAL SOLUTIONS

CONVERSATION MANAGEMENT

Evidence seems to show that most of us literally do not know what we are talking about most of the time. The English language has possibly upwards of half a million words. The average person's vocabulary is estimated to hover around only 20,000 words, and most people use less than 1,500 of these in their daily life—*plus* we "recycle" approximately 80% of what we say through the employment of habitual "stock phrases."

Linguistic systems are in constant flux—anyone who has attempted to read Chaucer or Shakespeare knows firsthand how even one's first language can become foreign to itself—shedding meaning through word-borrowing, speaker errors, and the introduction of slang (i.e., words that are by design indecipherable to all but a chosen few, the verbal equivalent of a secret handshake). Understanding is complicated even more by ever-changing contexts and through irony—which allows a word to not only have more than one meaning, but also with given inflections to even indicate its own opposite (e.g., the word *bad* demarking something as good).

To ensure diplomacy, politicians are trained to manage conversations; to talk about what they want to talk about, not what the other person wants to talk about; to answer the questions they wish had been asked, not the questions that actually were asked (i.e., "the Broken Record method").

Similarly, teachers are taught to avidly avoid telling students that their answer is "wrong," but instead to simply redirect them to whatever different, endorsed information that the instructor would like them to absorb.

With negotiators, a commonly-cited truth is that he who commits to a numerical figure first, loses. Knowing this, skilled negotiators often have almost comically-protracted exchanges as they both skirt the other's question by posing questions of their own (i.e., "the Porcupine Technique").

Whether it is our official occupation or not, we all act as salespeople and/or diplomats (or war mongers, for that matter) in everyday life.

Antidote

In diplomacy, the key is to respond selectively. When we pause—first, to consider whether even to answer—we break involuntary patterns and slow down the still rapid-fire process.

In conflicted situations, our two default choices are:

1. To not say anything at all: Often, a good self-defense strategy when facing imminent danger is to think, as in a meditation, rather than to speak your outlook (e.g., "You will not hurt me—that will not happen"; "I am a good person and I deserve good things"; "This, too, will soon pass").

2. If we do *choose* to respond, to talk about something other than what the individual is trying to speak about: This second option is analogous, on a verbal level, to the "misdirection" technique that magicians use when getting audiences to look *away* from the trick (e.g., in reply to someone claiming "You don't like me, do you?", we might reply, "It's been one heck of a day, that's for sure. How are things with you?").

(27) CURIOSITY (DID *NOT* KILL THE CAT)

Curiosity is the cornerstone of other-centeredness and the basis of solution-orientation as well as future-, rather than past orientation. Furthermore, without curiosity, empathy is not possible.

Deliberate acts of violence, whether verbal, physical, or emotional, can only be committed when empathy is deficient.

Without questions, choices are denied or unrecognized, and the past is left to dictate outcomes in perpetuity.

Without some doubt, we are left vulnerable to our surroundings. The twisted trade of everlastingly infuriated parties is hypersensitivity resulting from their guesses as to others' thoughts and evaluations about them and how those make them feel (or more accurately what they "think" they feel), but correspondingly deep dismissiveness of and insensitivity to how others might be affected emotionally by them.

Antidote

A recommended practice when faced with stressful circumstances is to first ask ourselves a question (i.e., "entertain the absurd") *and* then to also ask the person who is part of the stressful situation a question(s), *both* before making any attempt to reply through statements at all. By asking questions first, instead of leaping to short-sighted and damning conclusions, we remain open, nonjudgmental, and information-oriented, and can become better able to keep the attention on *dialogue* rather than debate.

Since crisis usually emerges in flashes—microseconds, triggered by micro-factors—it is advisable, when facing a crisis, to take a second look and cross-check our perceptions and reactions so that we are less likely to lash out rashly, based on misperceptions or faulty interpretations.

It can be helpful to note that some people's outsides and insides are mismatched to the extent that what they exhibit externally (e.g., irritation) may be far different from what they are experiencing internally (e.g., enjoyment or interest).

The checks and balances of doing a double-take (or even a *triple* take!)—"thinking *before* we 'think'"—helps keep us more closely aligned with what we intend overall, casting away what we might irrationally "feel like doing" in some ephemeral, hot-headed instant. The quest is for moderately delayed responses and slow*er*-motion, considered rebuttals (if one is even worth bothering to make at all).

To turn a well-worn phrase, "*Do* think twice about it."

(28) VERBAL EXCRETION:
THE SAFETY VALVE

Our experiences require processing. What we take in must also have an outlet.

We are designed to rid ourselves of emotional waste through our mouths. That which does not find release from consciousness through words is instead stuffed into the unconscious, where pressure builds until it is finally discharged, indirectly and usually disproportionately, through the body in acting out behavior—for instance, slamming a door closed or punching a hole through the wall.

Antidote

Because people rarely speak and physically act out at the same time, it is usually best to keep participants in a conflict talking. Rather than getting them to "shut up," the hope is actually that they *will* speak, targeting what they feel and the choices that *are* available to them.

Asking "what" and "how" questions places them in the position of educator, since implicit in these kinds of questions is the conviction that they are already in possession of the answers, can control themselves, and that the situation at hand is resolvable.

By asking "what" and "how" questions, we advance the conclusion and resolution rather than providing refusal as an explicit alternative. What we are striving for is not an "either/or" equation, but an "or-or-*or*" structure with each provided option taking different routes, but ultimately leading to the same place (i.e., constructive versus destructive compromises and collaborations).

Three things must be in place for a successful communication to occur: hearing what is said, shared comprehension, and belief in the validity of the message. Fâilure on any one of these levels leads to a breakdown in the message being received as intended, or at all.

Paradoxically, often when an individual is speaking a second or third language, he or she is a more effective communicator than the "native" speaker. Why? Because the person who is most acutely aware of the obstacles inherent in conveying meaning through language is usually more likely to take responsibility and work harder at gaining mutual understanding.

Anybody who has ever traveled extensively in foreign countries has probably had the experience that though we may not be able to "talk" to someone, we are usually still able to communicate (e.g., find out where the bathroom is) and understand (e.g., what or who is being spoken of).

Not all obstacles are as obvious as two people speaking different tongues, but clearly no communication between any two parties is entirely impediment-free. In fact, due to discrepancies in personal vocabularies and pronunciation, linguists state that no two people on earth ever speak *exactly* the same language. Everyone possesses his or her own idiosyncratic dialect. When we speak "*close* enough" to alike, we are then enabled to potentially decode the majority of what another has said.

We are so complex in our mental processes that we can even get ahead of the message by engaging in meta-communications—that is, communications about communication, the convolution of talking about talking (e.g., "Is it okay with you if I ask you a question?)—and can potentially lose the content in the process.

If communication is an art, we are all finger-painters.

The reason why dogs are often such "good" and

intent listeners, with their ears erect and head tilted in order to hear better, is that although they have almost no idea of what we are ever saying, they remain vitally interested and toil earnestly to decipher it . . . most likely in the hope that it has something to do with food or going for a walk.

a) Listening

More than half of any communication is based not on what is said, but on what is actually heard (or not heard).

"I told you that" is a common, past-oriented refrain that indicates the self-centered basis of so many communications. What it translates into more exactly is this: "I made a vocal effort of some sort for you to understand what *I* wanted you to understand."

(In other words, I made noise with my mouth in your immediate vicinity. I *tried* to communicate, not I *did* communicate.)

Though speaking can be attempted, it is often unsuccessful.

Given that we have two ears and only one mouth, that our brains can process almost twice as many words per minute as even the *fastest* speaker can speak, that light travels 110 times more quickly than sound, and that an individual's receptive vocabulary invariably far exceeds his or her expressive vocabulary—all seem to point towards listening being much more vital to our survival than speaking. (The reason that our receptive vocabulary far surpasses our expressive vocabulary is due to the fact that language acquisition cannot occur without our ability to infer meaning passively from context. Thus, to learn to talk at all, we must first hear [i.e., be exposed to language in some way].) Every one of us, no matter how articulate, has greater ease with—though not necessarily more willingness—consuming language than producing it.

The drive to "say something" (i.e., "*any*thing") can reach its apex during especially grave situations, when in actuality there might be no "right" thing to utter—nonetheless, countless tragic gaffes° are made at such times (e.g., "At least you have two more," being a brutal faux pas frequently posited to parents who have just lost a child). No one person or thing is powerful enough to relieve trauma so easily, and hollow assurances, such as "It'll be all right," and "Everything is okay," actually tend to *compound* the heartache when not accompanied by specific reasons why and how things could improve.

But *listening* almost always remains a viable option, barred only when the other absolutely refuses to speak. And even then we can still potentially listen to his or her silence.

Antidote

Most people will not listen to us until we've listened to them.

Curiosity and questions (with the latter being the outward manifestation of the former) both play a vital function in this process. Often, we don't need to "say" anything at all, we just need to let the other person express whatever it is he or she needs or wants to say.

Largely what people seek is a witness to their experience. This witnessing has the impact of lessening painful stimulus (by "sharing the load"), as well as amplifying pleasurable moments. Whether an experience is good or bad, the first thing most people want to do is to disclose it—to "*tell* somebody about it."

b) Comprehending

It is not enough that others listen to us. They must also grasp what we have told them.

Another's understanding of what is "right" and yours may differ radically. My belief as to what "a little while" constitutes may be 97 times longer or 1,002 times shorter than yours.

The struggle for many speakers is not a lack of speech, but a poverty *of content* (i.e., too many words, too little meaning). This can be exemplified by someone who tells us a how "great" a restaurant or country they've visited is, but then proves patently unable to provide a solitary detail as to why it's special.

Worse yet, implicit in any subjective, vague, abstract communication is that whatever *I* meant is correct, and anything other than that is wrong or lacking in some way—a dependable recipe for controversy. Assumptions are simply hunches or blind-faith beliefs that are not necessarily born out of truth. Confusing what is subjective (an assumption or bias) with what is objective (physical reality) frequently leads to misunderstanding and conflict.

Antidote

The word *communication* itself derives from the act of "making common" (dating back thousands of years to the *pre*-Latin word "*ko-moin-I*"), through which the participants come to know the same thing in the same way.

We are verbal–cognitive animals with the ability to not *just* indicate (e.g., point, moan) but actually *tell*.

The more specific we are, the greater the likelihood that we will be understood. For example, a smoker could argue that she is "being cooperative," but it is very difficult to dispute the tangibility of whether her cigarette is lit or unlit in a nonsmoking area.

The larger the gap between another's and our own interpretation of a *seemingly* alike thing, the bigger the turmoil.

As a recipient, the hope is to move away from allegations such as "You didn't say *that*," to more calibrated and matter-of-fact reports like, "There was a misunderstanding of some sort as to what was said."

c) Believing

Lastly, one must believe that what another tells them is true. If the listener feels that the speaker is not a credible source, he or she will dismiss the information as if it had not been communicated at all.

This is why being genuine and honest (i.e., speaking from the heart or gut) often acts as the trump card over all other factors. Irascible people, whose approach normally could offend, might be more successful in some cases since others might sense that they are "just being who they (truly) are." Though its unmuted expression is not necessarily to be lauded, anger is rarely faked. Conversely, niceness is often posited as socially acceptable camouflage for what one *really* feels, a deceit that can come back to haunt us later in a riptide or "backstabbing" kind of way.

Antidote

Consistency is critical to people trusting that we mean what we say. If we have set limits previously, without follow-through, then there is even *less* reason than there was before that the individual will "take seriously" the message that we are now trying to communicate.

The only thing usually worse than a limit that is clearly called for not being set, is a limit *being* set and then not upheld.

Words are symbols. The more distanced they become from what they are supposed to represent (e.g., naming nuclear weapons "peacekeepers"), the greater the resulting unease, neurosis, and even psychosis. Basic trust is damaged by these discrepancies (i.e., things literally lack meaning) and confusion is fed.

Disorder leads to greater disorder. Most of us are influenced environmentally by social proof. If we see an alleyway strewn with litter, we are more likely to litter there than we would be elsewhere. If we find legions of cars parking in front of an "absolutely no parking" sign, we are less likely to suppose that particular prohibition (or any other in the vicinity) is valid.

It is best that we strive not to be "mean," but to mean what we say.

Possible pitfalls:

1. Because manipulative and highly subjective individuals are conniving and lack transparency, they very rarely trust the good intentions of others. Their own motives are so self-serving, that they remain corrupt *even* when basked in niceness and caring. And due to their self-centered tendencies and deficient boundaries, they tend to cynically interpret other's objectives as being identical to their own in their lack of authenticity (e.g., "He wouldn't be that nice unless he wanted something from me, or he's just a sucker").

2. One of the main failings of any legal or educational system is when the gap between the formal (the written: what is supposed to be) and informal (enforcement: the ways things actually are) becomes too great and the system is nullified (i.e., no longer believed).

㉚ REACTION BAIT:
THE TWO VERBAL INVITATIONS TO ANTISOCIALITY

Aside from explicitly obvious slurs, name-calling, abuse, and profanity, there are two main verbal tactics that people use instinctively to provoke one another: the pointed finger of "you" messages, and shifting or keeping the focus on what has already occurred (usually, whatever has gone "wrong").

a) "You" Questions and Statements

Almost all verbal provocation is based on the shift from "I" to "you." This move explicitly delineates, on a verbal level, the violation of interpersonal boundaries.

People in (more or less) rational states of mind mostly talk about "what"—for example, "What's going on?"

Angered people who are not yet directly abusive talk about themselves—for example, "No one is telling *me* anything!"

Abusing individuals focus their anger overwhelmingly on others—for example, "What's *your* problem?!"; "What are *you* looking at?!"

Any time another person speaks about us, there is a much greater chance that we will be impacted emotionally. Salespeople, propagandists, and pop song writers know this, which is why all of them religiously utilize "you" messages, focusing on the subject that *you* (and almost everyone else in the world) is most deeply concerned with: *your*self.

Projection is a natural byproduct of stress. It need not be taught or studied; we are born knowing how to project—how to push away or repel on a psychodynamic level, like an infant kicking out its arms and legs while squirming when irritated.

Those using "you" messages are hunting for reactions. If we accept the invitation, like blood to a shark, they will go in for the kill.

Our goal is to "play possum" or dead to the bear. It is not at all easy to play catch with someone who refuses to participate or even acknowledge that the ball has been thrown.

Antidote

Not only is it beneficial for us to reduce or discard any sense of duty that obligates us to *have* to accept certain challenges should they occur, it is even more helpful to *expect* them as inevitable components of human relations.

Rather than *feeling* the effects of "you" barbs, we can condition ourselves to *hear* them (i.e., to be conscious of their emergence and what their usage indicates interpersonally), and thereby they can actually *help* orient us to the role that we are being offered, but do not necessarily have to play, in this cycle of provocation/antagonization (i.e., "tit-for-tat").

b) Past Orientations: What's Done *Is* Done

The past makes us inactive.
The present reactive.
The future proactive.

Angered individuals invariably refer to what has already happened. If we become engaged in a discussion of the past, we too are bound to get caught in this historical quagmire, increasing our own sense of helplessness.

Arguments often occur, prejudice is built, vengeance is fueled, and depression resides—in the past. No matter how much we may be willing to talk about what has already happened, we cannot alter it.

So, unless these discussions are intended to provide solutions for the future, they have nominal worth.

If the past is what is used as the primary basis for determining our current action, we are left only to replicate or compound errors, like the high casualty rates seen when an army persists in using traditionally "correct" but now-obsolete and ill-fit military practices (e.g., an *overly*-disciplined squadron advancing in classic formation towards rag-tag guerilla fighters).

A past-oriented person is constipated by his or her undigested history which—like a person who chronically overeats—literally begins to bog down him or her and can even in time, kill them.

Those who "don't care," feel they have "no future," or "don't see what I've got to lose" are usually far more dangerous than someone who is explicitly threatening (yet may only be bluffing or indirectly asking for help), for they have become dislocated from their own future. To them, their prospects are bankrupt, and so we have almost no remaining leverage to influence them positively. They now not only feel like doing something, but, also, no longer have any reason left *not* to do it. It is not all that surprising that those in trapped states tend to regress since the experience so closely mirrors the impotence and all-enveloping dependency of infancy. There might not be a more accurate depiction of post-traumatic stress than the past's being all-too-present and constantly intruding upon any and every new experience.

What we might better focus on is what *can* be done, not what has already occurred—what is possible, not what isn't possible.

Antidote

With conversation management, all that can usually be done beneficially when encountering past orientations is to listen and empathize. Anything else will almost always draw us into arguments about what should've or did/didn't happen.

Our goal can instead be to aid the individual so that he or she begins to invest in solutions and alternatives by working from a progressive versus perfectionistic model. In a progressive model we focus on what is, not what isn't, achievable and feasible.

The past-oriented individual's idyllic, romantic vision has been shattered and they are suffering due to having lost their sense of what potentially could've been. No argument is necessary, traded instead for an acknowledgement of that person's frustration. In addition, it can be immensely helpful to suggest options that that individual cannot currently recognize, create themselves, or yet accept. Tolerance of their viewpoint is not to condone it. It is simply realistic—an acknowledgment of what *is*.

Who erred or *why* is not central. *How* we can fix the matter is a preeminent use of resources. For example, consider the wording: "Yes, clearly this hasn't worked out so well. Let's look at what we can do now, from this point forward, to improve things."

(31) THE TWO MAIN SENDING ERRORS

There are two main ways that people, despite the best of intentions, trip themselves up verbally when attempting to gain positive results: by using "I/me/mine" messages and "yes/no" questions.

a) "I/me/mine" Messages: The Root of All Ego

Since "you" messages are the primary bait *others* use to provoke *us*, it follows that our own use of references to self ("I/me/mine") preemptively does that work on the behalf of others, and ultimately fosters the equivalent result by placing the spotlight—from the start—squarely on us rather than "what."

Our "personal-reference index"—which is the number of times that we refer to ourselves in each communication—is an objective indicator of one's degree of self-focus. "I/me/mine" communications usually are born out of ego-orientation.

Revealingly, according to studies, the most frequently used word conversationally by almost everyone is "I," yet it is almost never actually required to be understood factually.

Antidote

The more balanced alternative to personal references is to talk about "what" versus "who." This can be done through the introduction of lost performatives—losing the overt references to the performers (i.e., the speakers), instead framing messages with impersonal (*it/that/what/this*) as opposed to personal (*I/you/me/my/mine*) pronouns.

By training ourselves to use impersonal pronouns, we interrupt the "I/you" dichotomy that leans so heavily toward blame, and we are challenged to be more creative in constructing our messages.

Rather than "getting personal", the objective is "to get *im*personal"—that is, factual.

Examples:

<u>Not</u> "Why did *you* do that?" *but* "*What* happened?"

<u>Not</u> "*I* know . . ." *but* "*This experience* seems difficult."

<u>Not</u> "*I* need *you* to sit down" *but* "*It's* important *that* everyone is seated."

b) "Yes/No" Questions: *Giving* Misgivings

Arising from socially-obligated behavior, "yes/no" questions are designed to illustrate that we are making few assumptions whatsoever, and also that we are relinquishing nearly all power to the other individual. In turn, the other is expected to not abuse this power, and will customarily do whatever we ask within reason. Through this ritual, we develop trust. For example, the social model is to pose a yes/no question such as "Would it be okay if I drop by sometime?", to which the recipient, if prosocial, overperforms and states something along the lines of "Oh, yeah, for sure. Come over *any*time."

When misapplied to asocial, involuntary encounters, "yes/no" questions unwittingly reinforce black/white, all-or-nothing thinking, and reduce our odds to, at best, a 50/50 prospect of achieving our desired result—odds that, notably, are no better than chance (i.e., not having done anything at all). The "yes/no" construction actually creates odds that are *worse than chance*, as these types of questions often coerce people prematurely into committing to a posture that they are then likely to feel compelled to remain consistent with and not revise (i.e., repetition compulsion born out of past orientation).

For instance, though well-intended, the question "Do you want to talk about it?" easily allows someone not to and "Are you going to cooperate?" *suggests* rebellion as if it were and is a suitable choice.

Antidote

The questions we ask irrefutably shape the answers we receive.

If we don't want someone to tell us "no," then we shouldn't offer it to them as an explicit option to begin with. Instead, it is advisable to eliminate the negatives from our questions by structuring them as "how," not "if," exchanges. Success is much more likely when the outcome of our pursuit is not weakened by graphic doubt (i.e., when "no" is not given as *one of only two* available and apparent answers), but optimistic in nature, and based on the implicit presupposition that what we seek is attainable and in agreement with the other.

Examples:

Not "Do you want to go out this Friday night?" *but* "Let's go out sometime."

Not "Are you feeling sad?" *but* "How are you feeling?"

Not "Is it okay with you if I ask you a question?" *but* "What's going on?"

(32) THE TWO DEFAULT ANCHORING WORDS:

STARTING FROM A MORE SOLID FOUNDATION

Sidestepping the "you/I" ricochet can be accomplished by breaking the automatic conversational anchoring of "you" (with its tendencies towards baiting and blaming) and "I" (which so frequently illuminates the individual's degree of self- versus other-centeredness). Eliminating these polarities also displaces the behavioral niches (i.e., the "opposites" born out of opposition), tendencies, and inevitabilities to which they give rise.

By training ourselves to begin utterances without these stereotyped, either/or poles, we can become available to ponder our way through the communication—to literally think prior to, or at least as, we speak.

Antidote

There are two primary "starting words" in constructive communication: the aforementioned *what* and *let's*. Remembering to begin with these two little words can help keep us out of the emotional traps that easily form in so many facets of personal relationships.

1. *"What"*: What *is* the question? "What" questions keep the focus on information, not evaluation. To ask a "what" question is to request that the person being questioned provide more specific details. Implicit in this type of question is a steadfast faith that the person *does* have the answer. This method is the surest way to move beyond intellectualization and/or anger and "get at" the deeper emotions that are giving rise to them from beneath.

2. *"Let's"*: Use of *let's* not only reunifies the you/I split, it also bypasses the two primary traps of those sending information: both the "yes/no" questions as well as the "I/me/mine" statements, too.

It is not about *me*, it's about *we*.

By remembering what *to do* (and say), little attention need be given to what *not* to do.

(33) THE TWO ARGUMENT TRAPS

People usually fight when they believe that they are right. By appreciating that the other person probably also believes that he or she is right (and that that's probably a big part of the reason why they are fighting to begin with), it can become clearer that we might do best to center on something other than *right*ness.

In sending information verbally we can focus on facts, not feelings, to rebalance some possible effects of our arousal. When receiving information, it is best to invert this, instead honing in on identifying the speaker's feelings rather than debating facts.

If we are not extra-careful, often we can end up caught in a crossfire between them and someone/something else that isn't even there (e.g., something they are already mad about which then drives them to go "looking for a fight").

a) Listeners: Focusing on *Facts* Instead of *Feelings*

When people are upset, they almost always mostly express what they are feeling emotionally. In doing so, they tend to state things in a sloppy and extreme form—for example, "You *never* listen to me." Since these immoderate, absolustic statements are undoubtedly not entirely inaccurate, the receiving party usually reflexively begins to debate the accuracy of the information, which then only extends the void between them since the other's dealing with information probabilistically undercuts the significance of what the speaker is feeling and proves quite clearly that what they are *trying* to communicate *is truly not* being heard.

Antidote

In our listening, it is usually best to focus on feelings rather than facts. If we genuinely listen to the individual nonjudgmentally, much of intensity will usually subside. Note: There are few surer signs that someone feels that they are not being heard then when they raise their voice in an attempt to overcome the perceived barrier.

Similar to the above, hostage negotiators are trained to speak neither of the hostages nor the perpetrators' weapons, but instead to focus on the motivations and desired goals that drove the captors to arm themselves—that is, the negotiators focus on causes (i.e., the captors' emotions) instead of symptoms (i.e., their behavior), and almost never on what they don't want the captors to do (e.g., "No matter what, please don't harm the hostages" usually acts like a foregone conclusion that gunfire will sound like thunder after lightning).

Though what another is saying or doing may be undeniably disagreeable, his or her feelings need not be in debate.

Possible pitfall: Knowing something on an intellectual level is not enough and can even entrap us with an erroneous sense of self-assuredness. In order for our knowledge to be utilized and have applicable meaning, we must also *understand*. For example, I may know all of the facts and reasons why cigarettes are bad for me, but until I *fully* understand (i.e., feel) that they will kill me—and how that will, also, severely damage all those I love in the process—my behavior is unlikely to change.

b) Speakers: Overstating via "All-or-Nothing" Language

When we overstate our case, the receivers sense—whether unconsciously or consciously—that what we've said is not *entirely* accurate. Due to this, their focus shifts away from what we *were* attempting to communicate, to instead its factual soundness.

Antidote

Specificity, when accurate, increases the likelihood that what we are stating will be believed, or at least considered, instead of contested.

The more specific we are, the stronger the prospects that we will achieve mutual understanding. Erring on the side of understatement, in the long term, builds up our social equity by demonstrating that we are careful and thoughtful in our proclamations and don't promise what we later prove unable to deliver.

The power of preciseness and focus is demonstrated by the frequently studied truth that if you desire to gain assistance from a group, it is best to address specific individuals (who will usually then feel obligated to act), versus the entire group collectively (which usually results in dissipating responsibility among the assembled to the point of inaction).

㉞ DEFENSE-SOFTENING MECHANISMS

Regularly, the mistake is made of shaming the already shamed individual. Attacking somebody who already feels condemned or attempting to seize power from those who are not even in control of themselves almost always backfires.

Antidote

There are two "Trojan horse" words that defy people's expectations and interrupt reflexive, adversarial patterns: *okay/alright* and *unfortunately*. The cognitive dissonance these produce leave the receiver little choice but to reconsider his or her parameters and presumptions.

1. *Okay/alright*: These words explicitly indicate emotional agreement and a willingness to ponder a broader range of outlooks. They are not acceptances of the factual truth, but recognitions of the other's emotional commitment to them.
2. *Unfortunately*: Uttering this single word displays empathy explicitly. Its use is not a confirmation of the rightness or wrongness of what the other person is feeling, but, instead, an acknowledgment of his or her outlook. Note: This word can never be used factually; its existence is exclusively for attitudinal purposes.

Additionally, it can be useful sometimes to feed back to people their own *exact* word choices (versus just paraphrasing), since doing so explicitly mirrors them. This "mirroring" can help build a bridge of communication and connection whereby the individual recognizes that he or she is being both heard and understood.

This is particularly effective with overly concrete thinkers—that is, those who have difficulty interpreting beyond the superficial and obvious levels to instead envision the world around them as multidimensional and interrelated. Specifically, this can be the ability to learn from another's mistakes versus having to make the same mistake ourselves, or with empathy, the quality of understanding what another feels as perhaps being similar to what we too have experienced, even though they are undoubtedly not *identical*.

A successful outreach calls not for an increase in vigor (doing more of the same), but rather a change of modality entirely (doing something markedly different than that which was previously being done).

㉟ THOUGHT INOCULATION

In order for people to embrace new concepts or methods, it is first necessary that they concede—at least implicitly—that what they had been doing/thinking previously is less than perfect. The longer we have done something, customarily the more pronounced our conservatism and resistance to change (i.e., an orientation that is *again* stuck in the past). This is where experience can work *against* us.

Not *how long* but *how well* we've performed is a more relevant factor.

For eons, political and religious movements have known that assimilation is much easier than conversion. If a "new" ideology can ride on the coattails of an already existing group and belief system, then most of the toil has already been done. For example, colonialists often elect to observe holidays on the exact same date as preexisting ones, then incrementally alter the meaning of what they are commemorating, with the change occurring so gradually that it advances almost unnoticed and, therefore, goes largely unchallenged.

Antidote

A favored method for bypassing people's mental opposition and garnering their cooperation (i.e., hypnosis) is to present new ideas as if they were already their own. By disengaging from our pride and placing the concern on distribution of information, not attribution, we can make use of "awareness predicates" (e.g., words such as *notice*, *experience*, *aware*, *know*, *realize*). These types of words evoke less apprehension because they are presented with the confidence that the receiving individuals are already aligned and independently acquainted with the concepts being touted.

Additionally, individuals can be "paced" by first stating something with which the listeners are already in unity with and *then* linking that known idea to whatever it is the speaker hopes that they will now embrace (e.g., "The future of our children is of paramount importance, and that is why _____").

It is almost always easier to increase rather than decrease intensity. Thus, approaching someone gently reserves a wider field of options than "coming on too strong," whereby we paint ourselves (and them) into a corner. Prepping propositions with statements such as "There is no need to say 'yes' or 'no' right now, this is just maybe something to ponder" eases pressure and, paradoxically, inspires many people—particularly control freaks, who are so compulsively obstinate—to commit right away (since it is then *their* choice to make that on-the-spot agreement). It also eases pressure for perfectionistic people-pleasers to commit disingenuously.

In building bridges of accord and conciliation, it can be useful to note that very rarely do philosophical disparities pertain to *diagnoses* (i.e., that something is wrong). People's divergences are almost always based on *prescriptions* (i.e., what should be done about whatever is "wrong"). Unfortunately, those who provide an accurate diagnosis (i.e., identifying the problem) are often entrusted with providing a solution. Yet, the reality is that even toddlers can sometimes provide apt diagnoses (i.e., knowing when circumstances are not right), but this in no way lends them—or anyone else for that matter—any expertise to prescribe.

(36) HYPHENATED-IDENTITIES

Though not necessarily problematic in and of itself, almost everyone's identity is hyphenated. Very few think of themselves as just a human, but more likely, also, as a "man" or "woman." Almost none of us stops short at just a single adjective. Instead, we are a young/adult/elderly/etc.-woman/-man. And this process only enlarges from there, threading a conceptual string.

Though we may not be able to articulate it, we are likely to view ourselves in terms of some lengthy, hyphenated descriptor—for example, as a "mature-smart-attractive-athletic-tough-modern-American-woman"—or something along these lines, with an order, emphasis, and composition that fluctuates daily, if not hourly.

Antidote

The trick is to introduce new notions and options in a way that is nonthreatening and not seen as contradictory, but instead as congruent with, and reinforcing of that person's (or our own) existing self image For example, "Yes, you *are* a strong person. And real strength requires being able to _____."

Rather than subtraction (of the "bad" element), we are implementing addition (of the new adjective), which will hopefully, in time, whittle away at or displace entirely any targeted undesirable behavior. Doing this, yet again, is another way to help reinforce what we want versus what we don't want.

PATTERN INTERRUPTION

If what we are doing isn't working, it becomes advisable to do something else. Waiting for others to change instead leaves us at the mercy of externalities.

The reason that even extreme diets and Draconian mental health interventions "work" (i.e., have impact and show results initially) is that they serve to disrupt the preexisting design, albeit in dire ways.

Under the false impression that we see all of what is around us, we miss the fact that we actually see only that which we *do* see. Our attention is, by necessity, selective. If we attended to everything in our midst, we would quickly be fraught by the deluge of stimuli and unable to attend to *anything* at all (i.e., which has frequently been cited as the most accurate description of the experience people have while in floridly psychotic states). That is why our automatic filters manage most potential stimuli by blocking them from registering in our consciousness to begin with.

We all have limited attention and energy. That to which we devote energy or attention reduces or eliminates what else we can attend to or accomplish. By focusing on troubles or on that which is beyond our sphere of influence (i.e., things we cannot change), we set ourselves up for aggravation.

We cannot control our circumstances, but we can potentially control ourselves. By doing this (i.e., a form of "the unexpected"), we produce cognitive dissonance in others, motivating them to think and reevaluate us as *individuals*. Otherwise, we risk falling into the mutually-damaging trap of having someone treat us as if we were a bad person and then behaving like one in reaction.

On a larger and more pervasive level, when an authority figure or culture not only *doesn't* discourage but actually celebrates an unfit behavior, it will propagate until reaching the point where it becomes normalized and is established as the new (*sub-*)standard—for example, rudeness or selfishness being misidentified as funny, tough, or courageous.

Rather than being encouraged to connect with it, some people might do better getting *out of touch* with their inner child.

Antidote

A good practice is to train ourselves to look *away* from any obvious and extreme thing that immediately grabs our focus (i.e., where the "action" is), and instead scan our surroundings and observe whatever else might not be so readily apparent.

Often, the most tried-and-true method for disrupting undesired patterns is to do the very *opposite* of what we feel like doing or normally would do (e.g., to admit and talk about what we are feeling rather than withdrawing and "clamming up").

That which attracts our instant attention does so because it is interesting (. . . at least, to us). But, conversely, anything we eagerly give attention to generally becomes more intriguing through the act of concentration itself. More than breeding contempt, familiarity has a propensity to generate enhanced appreciation and understanding.

Possible pitfall: Those with histories of unhealthy relationships frequently become uncomfortable the longer that things continue to go right. Unconsciously, their tendency is to sabotage ties with those who treat them well, in an effort to return to their tried-and-true "comfort zone" *of discomfort*. Frequent and brief contacts (part of a larger *process*) versus intense and lengthy encounters (attempting to have a one-time transformative *event*) usually are more thriving. They allow the individual to learn more slowly, in stages, to trust the new reality of a positive bond and that he or she need not be betrayed "like *all of* the other times."

㊳ MUTUAL TRANSFORMATION

Erroneously, people are often viewed more or less as inanimate objects upon whom experiences have one-way effects, meaning that those results are unchangeable (e.g., considering oneself to be psychologically or emotionally "scarred").

As living beings we are not only being acted on, but also are acting upon all that we encounter. Rather than requiring a strict diet of set elements, our consciousness has the ability to use whatever it is supplied as grist.

We need not just passively receive circumstances; rather, we can actively engage the world and potentially modify *it* in the process.

Whoever inherits (or steals) the first right of interpretation about an event wields the highest power of persuasion, pioneering the precedent-making spin and template that will reverberate through and possibly misguide the course of subsequent definitions and perceptions (e.g., the hysteria that can be set off by a single person sounding a false alarm or lodging a fraudulent accusation).

Antidote

We have little control over what happens around us, but almost *complete control over how we respond to it.* The goal is metabolization of our experiences. How can we help facilitate this? By following these two steps:

1. Admitting what we feel, regardless of how we would like to feel differently.
2. Finding a proper outlet for those emotions (usually verbal).

Among the tragic side effects of judgmental and rigid atmospheres is that by discouraging dialogue, they produce dishonesty. If only one answer can ever be the correct one, it is likely that we will be reluctant to speak at all. And if the few communications that are then ever even risked are met with hostility and rejection, it becomes increasingly probable that an individual will begin bending the truth to appease such an unyielding and harsh audience.

Note: The highest suicide rates globally are found in shame/honor-based nations that place an inordinate value on stoicism.

(39) THE IMPORTANCE OF ACCURACY

Drifts and distortions of truth often occur with the exaggerated and wholesale agreements that tend to "ride for free" when parties concur about something *else*. In other words, if someone is "on our side" (or is meeting some other need for us) we often passively condone and tolerate other opinions and ideas that we might otherwise dispute, as long as he or she "goes along" with the larger agenda. This compromising of truth can eventually lead to radicalization and the subreality of groupthink—that is, erroneous ideas that gain a sense of legitimacy due to collective belief—with "the more the merrier" being key.

(Additionally, so many human errors are based on romantic, wishful, and imprecise mathematics, whereby one minimizes the number of calories or amount of alcohol they've consumed, how fast they drive, or the true tally of their credit-card bill, all of which would benefit from greater precision to help ward off avoidable regrets down the line.)

Antidote

Monitoring for and actively working towards accurate representations of reality helps strengthen our communications. Building a subtle, more fully factual, colorized environment of trust where disagreement is possible allows us to refine our thoughts and correct any missteps or overreaches in ideation that might occur when we are too zealous. For example, consider the perpetual, generational reactionism of statements like: "Teenagers *these* days are *totally* out of control. What we need to do is put surveillance cameras in every single classroom!"

It can prove wise to be on the lookout that we don't pardon inappropriateness by way of our acquiescence, which is apt to happen when alliances coalesce on a nonpositive basis (e.g., siding with the lesser of two evils), and ushered piggyback on the shoulders of a common enemy, that is, whenever my desperation for "help" pushes me to concede values and truth.

Total agreement can be too much of a good thing.

⑩ LIMIT-SETTING AS EDUCATION

Limits on others are customarily placed puni-
tively as well as judgmentally (implicit in them
is that the "wrongdoer" should have already known
"better").

A more profitable approach can be to regard limits as educational and beneficial for everyone, *most
of all the person on whom the limits are being placed*.

Tell people what to do, and they will rebel.

Ask them "if" they would like do something, and
they will refuse (no less than half the time).

Issue a challenge, and they are likely to stubbornly
undertake it and become combative.

However, educate them as to *what* the reasons are
that it is in *their* best interest to do what is being sug-
gested, and they will usually embrace it, even when
you are no longer present, because they are not
doing it for you, they are now doing it for themselves
(as well they *should* [irony intended]). The unnecessary broker (i.e., you) has been cut out of the deal,
displaced by pure data and self-motivation.

Antidote

Limits work well when framed as helpful reminders, not as recriminations. Ultimately, we are creating, not "setting" limits. This creation of limits is a collaborative act, for if the other person does not abide by our suggestion, then the endeavor is all but just short of worthless. But if a person does consequently alter his or her behavior, then together we have created something new that did not exist before our joint efforts.

Precedents *do* take precedent, or, at the very least, sway the interpretation of whatever else follows (i.e., another corrupting facet of past orientation). Statistically speaking, the most powerful placement of anything we say is that which is said first. That is why it is so important to start positively and "say something good, before we say anything bad." If the first thing out of our mouths repels, often the person will stop listening at all.

We can anticipate resistance and a backlash to any disruption of another's drive. Often, though, what we are witnessing is simply the death throes and last gasp of what existed before—akin to the supernatural strength people frequently exhibit when wounded or dying—and once there is time to recalibrate and "cool down," the new information may actually be surprisingly well-heeded (e.g.,

"Now that I *think* about it, maybe you were right after all").

In a world of carrots and sticks (i.e., rewards and punishments), the optimal approach is to use *both*—with each balancing the other, and the latter reserved only as a last resort for exceptional cases. Sticks are almost never inspirational, but only corrective, after the fact. They rarely stop people before the event—since most times the person isn't thinking at that point anyway—but only have any value later (e.g., catching or punishing the criminal who has *already* committed the crime).

Possible pitfalls:

1. More than being "friendly" (a social model sometimes misappropriated by those in leadership roles), a most loving and kind act is to adequately prepare someone for, and approximate the feedback and consequences that they are most likely to receive, in the "real" world.
2. There may be secondary gains (i.e., byproducts of the consequence) that could be unintentionally rewarding someone for his or her otherwise penalized conduct. For example, the child who is habitually "in trouble" since it is his or her only proven means for getting attention of any sort.

There are two main ways in which we can foster a process of healing with challenging and challenged persons; via appeals to their health and by stressing progress over perfection.

a) Appeals to Health

Even the unhealthiest individual has some healthy components to his or her personality. No one behaves consistently across every circumstance. For example, the corporate-raiding attorney might be a shrinking violet or even the *victim* of abuse at home. The most violent relate to a privileged few not with harm, but with protection. It is comforting to note that even the most aggressive individuals in the world spend the vast majority of their time not being physically violent (literally, far less than 1 percent of the time). Still more comforting is the consistent data from multiple studies that have shown that even *among* violent criminals, less than 6 percent of them can actually be categorized clinically as "sadistic."

In other words, the great majority of violent individuals do not enjoy, and in some cases even regret, their own violent actions. Instead, they usually only become violent when they feel they have no other choice—and that sense of having no other choice occurs in direct relationship to absolustic thinking.

Stunningly, even Hitler believed he was acting in

"defense" by invading neutral countries and executing millions of his own citizens. It is often overlooked that paranoia itself is a form of grandiosity—the belief that people . . .

1. are aware of us at all

   and

2. that we are important enough for them to even bother trying to harm us.

It is not that most people are benevolent; rather, they are simply indifferent. Every person has a finite amount of energy, and furthermore, most criminal individuals lack discipline and are fundamentally lazy, which forms a sizeable component as to why they search for the "short cuts" of cheating interpersonally in the first place.

From a prediction standpoint, the most sobering, by far, are the elite few that have come to celebrate and enjoy the pain of others.

Almost all individuals who become violent attack with victim-specificity. They are selective, to the point of often being formally "prejudiced" about whom they injure.

In the final analysis, though, all violent individuals attack the same target: whomever they feel deserves it.

That's a primary reason why it is so vital that we overperform in an effort to be above reproach.

There are almost 7 billion people on the planet. They have better people to kill than you, so don't give them a reason to do it.

Some people's target is so narrow and precise that they may reserve all their rage for only their most intimate partner (whom they use as a sort of personal dumping ground), and otherwise function at the extremity of being an irrepressible people-pleaser with everyone else, often misapplying love especially tirelessly towards those that mistreat *them* the most.

Nobody is the same person with every person. There is variance even among the most steady. The majority of us evaluate ourselves based on our optimal behavior, while others' regard for us may only be founded on having witnessed us at our "worst" (e.g., when frustrated while going through airport security). Ethical behavior is strongest when we are marginally affected by our audience, behaving in the same fashion whether we are being watched or not watched, punished or rewarded. But few are that pure (e.g., there are few among us who do not slow down if we see a police car trailing us).

Antidote

Rehabilitation appeals to the healthy, not unhealthy, aspects of the individual—transcending the negatives *even when* they are the more palpable, immediate, and active quality.

We can do this by focusing on what we want, not what we don't want, from others that are struggling.

What we hope to connect with is the interior of their moral circle—no matter how tiny—the destruction-free zone where it is no longer us versus them, but where there is only "us."

It is valuable to bear in mind that creation and destruction stem from the same yearning: to have impact. Indeed, the amount of resources that antisocial people devote towards devious ingenuity could cure most of the world's ills if properly channeled. Though the appeal of destruction is understandable given its relative ease and accessibility to all (e.g., it may take a master painter years to complete a canvas, some malcontent can destroy it with one clumsy slash of a knife), the wish is for those that are so inclined to discover the intrinsic and *further*-reaching rewards of constructive activities.

The presence of energy of any sort can potentially be viewed positively. For example, often it turns out that ultimately the identified "problem child" in a family is actually the healthiest, because he or she is usually the member most tacitly aware of what he or she is feeling, as well as being willing to ardently admit—albeit in less than desirable ways—that something is awry. The challenge is to redirect those energies in a more fruitful manner. Similarly, the forecast is often much better for someone who discloses, "I have a short fuse, for sure," contrary to another who alleges, "I don't get angry."

It is better to remain concerned with what another is able, not unable, to do.

In terms of our own ethics, since the video camera has largely replaced "God" as the all-seeing eye, a good rule in keeping ourselves earnest is to avoid engaging in any activity that we would not want others to review later, at their leisure, with adjustable speeds, and with the utmost detail.

Possible pitfall: Nobody likes to fail. Ironically, this is why some people commit to failure so fully, since it is the one surefire thing that they can succeed at. This tends to occur particularly when the bar for success has been set almost unreachably high, which can lead to not-uncommon counterproductive conclusions such as, "I may not be able to ever be a doctor, like mom and dad, or a star athlete like my brother, but I sure as hell can be the biggest (i.e., 'the best') fuck-up this family's ever seen."

b) Progress versus Perfection

The perfectionistic model is a hypercritical one that leads to repeated frustration due to its inaccurate depiction of the world.

By focusing on progress rather than perfection, we can meet individuals *wherever* they are aand begin leading them back to where we want them to go or where they "should" be.

When working from a progressive model, the "worse" the behavior is, the more liberated we become and the better off we are in the sense that at low points or "rock bottom," options are at their most plentiful. Almost *any*thing is an improvement relative to what a troubled individual is currently doing or about to do. If someone is on the verge of killing him- or herself, whether he or she is catastrophically in debt or is an addict is of little "big picture" concern at *that* moment.

Antidote

Nearly all positive developments, no matter how slight, can genuinely be encouraged. Opportunities for accord (e.g., pockets of agreement), even though miniscule and hidden, are seldom unavailable. Emphasizing these harmonies interrupts the adverse momentum of argumentative or unsympathetic exchanges and frees possibility.

Idealists stumble when they insist on only clear-cut choices between "good/bad" and "right/wrong." Encouraging others to maturely evaluate and commit, even when facing two of life's most common predicaments—that of having to elect between two undesirable ("lesser of two evils") or two or more attractive options (not being able to "have your cake and eat it too")—can lead to an elevated tolerance for ambiguity and to the integration of good and bad into one indivisible continuum.

Contrastingly, a rare instance in which totalities (all-or-nothing language) can be used beneficially is in communicating acceptance of whatever another (or we ourselves) is feeling.

Possible pitfall: The word "problem" often creates one.

What we are experiencing need *not* be a problem. Instead, it can *potentially* be nothing more than a solvable, briefly disruptive, mildly frustrating, and ultimately forgettable blip on the radar of life.

AFTERWORD

The humble hope is that this book *might* prove able to help *some* individuals *some*, though *probably* not all, of the time.

Accepting that not *all* situations are preventable allows us to concentrate on the vast majority of those that are, and hopefully also helps inhibit our confusing that which is difficult with that which is definitively (and, thankfully, very rarely) impossible.

It's not "*all* good," but it is *mostly* good.

Revealingly, America is the only culture that regularly speaks of being in *control* without specifying *of what*. This typifies the empty aspiration to be in control of *every*thing. The real trick is to accept how very little we are ever actually in control of . . . save for *potentially* ourselves.

Recognition of the capacity for both good and bad deeds in all individuals, along with the admission of our own limitations and negative potential, can provide proper motivation to take preemptive, constructive action (i.e., stopping a crisis before it happens) rather than gambling with outcomes and shirking accountability.

If all people were treated with the same respect as the largest and scariest, and if every person were granted forgiveness equal to that afforded the tiniest infant, few miscalculations would be made.

By framing interactions in terms of mutual benefit and not competition, much of the doom can be relieved from otherwise neutral situations that are incited due to a misguided sense of winning or losing.

Truly, we *are* all in this together.

APPENDIX

a) Conflict Resolution at a Glance for Those on the Run

People act out negatively mostly due to fear. This fear is masked by anger to protect the ego, which may be threatened in addition to any physical danger that's actually present.

We provoke others by talking . . .

1. About them (e.g., via "you" statements and questions)
2. About the past (e.g., "They always let me park here.")

The most common unintended speaker missteps are . . .

1. Referring to ourselves ("I/me/mine")
2. Using "yes/no questions," which are based on *at least* a fifty-percent negative expectation

People become violent when they feel that they are right. Arguing with them factually, instead of identifying with them emotionally, only intensifies the separation and sense that we are "wrong" and against them.

Humans are predisposed to reciprocate behavior, so generally we get back whatever we give out. The most effective use of our energy in positively influencing others is to control ourselves instead of trying to control them—which they will almost always rebuff.

The greater the opportunity to become violent (e.g., an available weapon, an isolated environment), the more likely it is to occur. When people act out violently, they are less rational than when they are not violent. This is why intoxication so often plays a part in these situations.

Nevertheless, we can almost always stimulate *some* rational thought by . . .

1. Asking questions ("what" and "how," *not* "if")
2. Giving options

Providing choices to others places them in a leadership role, thereby encouraging self control as well as counteracting their sense of helplessness.

Extremes of some sort—from the obvious to the covert—usually play a part in creating crisis situations.

Black/white thoughts and language lead to all/ nothing outcomes and perceptions that rarely reflect the greater complexity of a situation and that then lead to cruder evaluations, with resultantly blunt behaviors.

We can strive for balance by staying open to possibilities and progress, and by speaking about *what* is happening versus to *whom* it is happening.

b) Instantaneous Self Check-Up:

TWO VITAL THINGS TO ASK IF WE FIND OURSELVES ANGERED

1. "Do I really want to choose to allow this person into (*or more deeply into*) my life? (especially if he or she is likely to hijack or ruin it in the process.)"

2. "Is this person really more important to me than myself, my goals and/or my loved ones?"

c) Bottom-Line Violence Prevention Quotes & Slogans

Though some of these may seem a bit trite and/or "cutesy," they can potentially help encapsulate, as well as strengthen recall of, some meaningful concepts.

"Self control is the crossroads of crisis."

"Do *not* do unto others as they do unto you."

"It's not about *me*, it's about *we*."

"Don't be 'mean,' but *mean* what you say."

"It is almost impossible to argue with someone who is agreeing with you."

"If we don't know what to say, the best thing to 'say' is usually nothing at all and, instead, to simply listen (. . . and, hopefully, think)."

"Peace to all, harm to none."

"We don't have to win every battle. Truth is, we probably aren't even at war to begin with."

"If we are living in a 'dog-eat-dog world,' it's of *our* own making—dogs *don't* eat dogs."

"Even better than not being in the wrong place at the wrong time is to not be there in the first place."

"The word 'might' is *mighty*."

"If things going the way they 'should' acts as our gauge for whether or not to explode, then we better be braced for a lifetime of pyrotechnics."

"Almost no one ever *'makes'* us do anything that we don't choose to do ourselves."

"Prison walls are filled almost exclusively with convicted 'victims'—victims of circumstances, victims of the system, victims of *every*thing, but, most of all, themselves."

"*Some*, but not *all*, is almost always the proper sum."

"Maybe, more than 'being a man,' be *human*."

"If it's too good to be true, it probably isn't really true."

"Ironically, much dishonorable behavior comes from people trying to defend their honor."

"Those who can't control themselves attempt to control others. But control others and you will without fail eventually be controlled."

"Our anger is *our* problem, much more than anyone else's. Few benefit from losses of self control. Those who suffer most are often the ones who've 'lost it.'"

"There is no surer way for people to unintentionally reveal *who* they are than by claiming *what* they are not."

"Being 'right' doesn't help us in a crisis situation. You can be right and still get your ass kicked. It happens to people every day."

"It's not '*all* good,' but it is *mostly* good."

"If we feel stuck, often the best solution is to try the exact opposite of what we are considering or are doing presently."

"Asking 'yes/no questions' gives us no better odds of getting what we want than chance (i.e., doing nothing at all)."

"If communication is an art, we are all finger-painters."

"We should almost always first attempt to say something good before we say something bad."

"Ignore the behavior, not the individual."

"Don't argue with the facts, agree with the feelings."

"One person may have 'started it,' but it almost always takes two to finish it."

"When encountering an overly judgmental, perfectionistic individual, try as hard as we might, we are all found guilty as charged: of the crime of being human."

"No one is the same person with everyone. Even the most violent individuals in the world spend 99.99 percent of their lives *not* being violent."

"The vast majority of people on the planet earth are not benevolent, just indifferent. They have better people to kill than you, so don't give them a reason to do it."

"If we do not learn to live with the imperfections of others, we condemn ourselves to a hell of our own making, for we are not living in the world that we've been given."

"Violent individuals are unrelenting accountants, accounting for everything *but* the consequences of their own behavior."

"History is almost always smarter than we are. Repetition is the single most reliable predictor of future behavior."

"Rather than being encouraged to, some people might do better getting *out of touch* with their inner child."

"Whatever we start, we may not be able to finish—but it may finish us."

"There is no 'us and them.' There is only us."

"Who among us is not a vengeful, perverted, suicidal, mass-murdering maniac in our heads? It is not the presence of an impulse that is a problem, it is the inability to control it."

"The mailmen get bitten because they keep going back."

"Instead of just loving your country, love your world."

"If you make policing the 'assholes' your job, you're going to be working overtime for the rest of your life, for no pay."

"When we 'lose control' of ourselves we almost invariably lose far more as a result."

d) Three and One-half Paradoxical Truths in Evaluating Others

1. Whatever you feel negatively in response to them, they likely feel themselves (e.g., the threatening individual who is actually afraid).

2. Whatever they claim they're "not," they might be.

a) Whatever they assert they are usually has *less* chance of being true than whatever else they do not profess.

3. Whatever they allege you are, *they* probably are.

e) Tact Building:

FOUR THINGS TO GENERALLY AVOID SAYING TO OTHERS

1. What you *don't* want them to do.
2. What they could've done, but now can't.
3. Asking *if* they want to do something.

4. Telling them that they or their situation is "exactly" like anything else (which places conditional value on them and positions ourselves in the unsolicited role of judgment).

f) Two Big Myths in Crisis Situations

1. **"There was no warning."** *No warning* translates into, that there was no obvious or spoken warning. Just because someone didn't express him- or herself verbally rarely means that something wasn't shown or revealed.

2. **"I didn't do anything."** Though we didn't *say* anything, that certainly doesn't mean that meaning or feelings weren't transmitted. We are never *not* communicating. "I didn't do anything" is often used to put forth the absolustic defense, "I didn't do anything that deserved *this*."

g) Ideological Restructuring:

THREE INTERNAL MESSAGES TO MONITOR, INTERRUPT, AND MODIFY

1. "I can't _____," rebalanced by, "It is difficult for me to . . ."

2. "I am/am not_____," rebalanced by, "Overall, I have/have not tended to be . . . "

3. "I never/always _____," rebalanced by, "Most of the time I have.../Rarely have I . . . "

h) Ways to Identify a Polluting Personality in Your Midst

1. Their conflicts are not isolated, but repeated with numerous individuals.
2. We find ourselves spending an inordinate amount of time thinking and talking about them.
3. Almost every encounter with them results in our feeling diminished afterwards.
4. They seem to view other's success as threatening and personalize most encounters.
5. Cooperation and/or following simple directions is identified by them as weakness and therefore almost any action that they've not themselves initiated is resisted.
6. They dismiss things that they do not comprehend or agree with as "stupid" or "ridiculous."
7. They frequently attempt to enlist others to take sides in matters, involving those who otherwise would not be and thereby widening the controversy.

i) (Subtler) Warning Signs: *Some* Instant Red Flags

1. People who try to tell you what you should feel (e.g., "Come on, it's a party, be lively!").
2. Those who, upon first meeting, feel compelled to inform you "what kind of person you *are.*"
3. Someone who likes you too much, too soon. What goes up, must come down. We probably won't have to wait indefinitely for the other shoe to drop on this ardor.
4. Others who want to compare us to others (i.e., past orientation, e.g., "You are *exactly* like my friend, Joe."). Their evaluations and boundaries are transparently crude at best.
5. Virtually any time someone is unlike anyone that ever we've met before, there is a reason—for well or naught. When feeling uneasy, listening to, though not necessarily acting on, our gut instinct and "tip-of-the-tongue" edge of consciousness will rarely mislead us.

j) Constructive Communication's Least-Wanted Words

(*Note*: The word *the* is often an accomplice, aiding the other absolutes.)

Just/Only	"I was *just* saying. . . ." "I *only* had one beer."
. . . too	"She was doing it, *too*."
Is/are	"He *is* a total jerk." "You *are* such an asshole."
Should	"They *should* know better."
If	"*If* you really loved me, you would _____."
Unless	"No one would do that, *unless* they were a complete asshole."
But	"You're a great guy, *but* . . ."
Make/made	"You *make* me so angry." "He *made* me do it."
Have/had	"I *have* to show him who's boss." "I *had* to put her in her rightful place."
Can't	"I *can't* let people get away with that shit."
Not	"That's *not* the way the world works."
Most/-est	"That is the *most* stupid thing ever." "He's the bigg*est* asshole."
Best/worst	"He was the *best/worst* boss in the world."
Always/never/all	"You *always/never* do that." "You say that *all* of the time."
Nothing	"There is *nothing* anybody can do."

k) Energy:
THE SILENT LANGUAGE OF THE BODY

Five less-obvious things that can give us a "clue" about others:

1. *Elevation*: Things that rise tend to indicate positivity (e.g., the mouth and brow when we smile), and things that fall or shrink are generally indicators of negatives.
2. *Eye blocking*: Almost any gesture towards, or a narrowing of, the eyes is an indication of unwanted stimuli, even when and if it is internal in origin (i.e., a thought or memory versus that which is seen).
3. *Pacifying behaviors*: Most people will overcompensate when under stress by self-soothing (e.g., covering vulnerable areas such as their lower throat, wringing their hands, rubbing their thighs).
4. *Changes*: Regardless of whether it's an increase or decrease, almost all individuals will demonstrate a change of some sort when affected in a significant way emotionally.
5. *Intention cues*: People will almost always position themselves away or recoil from undesired stimuli and move or point themselves towards that which attracts them. Often, their body will be split, with the top half twisting to engage out of social obligation, but the lower half and feet (the furthest from the brain and the "most honest" part of the body, emotionally) oriented elsewhere.

I) Gentler Enforcement:

LIMIT-*CREATION* OVERVIEW

DO: Desired action can potentially be created through two easy steps.

1. Talk about what you want, not what you don't want, the other person to do.
2. Focus on *what* the other person is feeling or thinking, *not if* he or she will stop doing whatever he or she is doing.

DON'T: Most people make one of two common errors.

1. Tell the person what you don't want them to do, thus drawing attention to and even strengthening the prohibited behavior (e.g., "stop kicking that chair").
2. Ask them "yes/no" questions as to whether they will comply, thereby providing a too-easy opportunity to refuse.

The softening words—

Unfortunately: (demonstrates empathy without reference to self).

Okay/alright: Four things are accomplished simultaneously with these one-word agreements. They acknowledge . . .

1. That you've heard them.
2. That they believe what they are saying to be true.
3. That as unlikely as it might seem, it *could* be true.
4. Refusal to argue whether this is one of the rare cases where what they are saying is true.

The fallback words—

Let's: Includes others as part of the solution and presupposes positive action (i.e., not if but that they can and will engage in desired behavior).

What: As opposed to "why" questions, these seek information, not justification, for an action, thereby reducing defensiveness.

m) Common Conceptual Confusions

These false-friend imposters disturb balance by creating the illusion that a principle is being fulfilled when it isn't, or that it is not, when it is.

Mistaken glorifications:

Rudeness for toughness
Selfishness for courage
Histrionics for love
Arrogance for confidence
Apathy for calm
Conviction for righteousness
Aggression for assertiveness
Emotional honesty for truth
Cynicism for wisdom
Knowing (intellectually) for understanding (emotionally)
Callousness for strength
"Can't" for "don't want to"
"Have to" for "*choose* to"
"I don't know" for "I don't want to say"

Ambition for passion
Stealing for winning
Ruthlessness for smartness
Social obligation ("niceness") for kindness

Cynical demotions:

Compassion for weakness
Diplomacy for cowardice
Generosity for manipulation
Calm for fear
Shyness for arrogance
Optimistic for unrealistic
Doubt for unreliability
Different for wrong
Subpar for *the* worst
Mistakes for failure
Conflict for war
Difficult for impossible
Often for always
Rarely for never

n) Losing the Performers:

PUTTING "WHAT" BEFORE "WHO"

Examples of how to communicate in an impersonal (i.e., more neutral) style are shown in the following table and make use of five simple words: *it, that, what, this,* and *how.*

Personal versus Impersonal Styles of Communication	
"You/I" statements	**Factual substitutions**
"You're wrong."	"That's wrong."
"I've about had it with you."	"It might be best to talk about this later."
"You need to quiet down."	"It's very important that the volume remains low."
"I hate you."	"This is upsetting."
"Why did you do that?"	"What happened?"
"I understand."	"That's understandable."
"Fuck you."	"Fuck that."
"Can I help you?"	"How can we help?"

The goal of asocial encounters is to usurp the division of social "you/I" messages with impersonal pronouns (*it/that/what/this*) that place the focus on *what* is happening.

Graph of How to Get Impersonal in Your Communication			
Personal ⟶	⟶ ⟶ ⟶		Factual
"I think you are stupid."	"You are stupid."	"What you did was stupid."	"That probably wasn't the smartest thing ever."
"I know how you feel."	"You must be really upset."	"What are you feeling?"	"It's understandable that something like this might be upsetting."

o) Autopsy of a "You/I Ricochet"

Speaker A: "What can I do to help you?"

Speaker B: "You can't do shit."

Speaker A: "Hey, I'm just trying to help."

Speaker B: "Then leave me the fuck alone."

Speaker A: "There's no need for you to talk to me that way."

Speaker B: "I can talk to you any way I want."

Speaker A: "No, you can't."

Speaker B: "What are you going to do about it?"

Speaker A: "You don't want to find out."

Speaker B: "You know what? Fuck you."

Speaker A: "Fuck you, too, asshole."

This is hardly a transcript of a successful resolution. Sadly, and all too commonly, it is worsened by speaker B's inability to relinquish him- or herself as the prime topic.

If deliberate focus had been shifted to what Speaker A was experiencing as opposed to what Speaker B thought, then a better outcome might have resulted.

Speaker A: "What's going on?"

Speaker B: "You can't do shit."

Speaker A: "That may be true, but you certainly seem upset."

Speaker B: "I have every right to be."

Speaker A: "No one is questioning that, at all. What's up?"

Speaker B: "You know what, leave me the fuck alone."

Speaker A: "Okay. Clearly, what you're experiencing right now is very intense and that's totally understandable."

Speaker B: "No one understands what I'm going through. You don't understand."

Speaker A: "Okay. Well, let's talk about what is happening. You seem very passionate about it. What's going on?"

Speaker B: "Fuck you, man."

Speaker A: "Okay. If there's anything we can do to help, please let us know."

Although imperfect, this less-than-ideal result nonetheless boasts a modestly improved conclusion as far as exercising choice and refusing to reciprocate negatively even when repeatedly invitated to.

p) The Straitjacket of Manhood

I *can't* cry. I *have* to be strong.
Can't be weak.
Have to be tough. *Have* to be a man.
Can't take shit.
Have to be on guard . . . *always*.
Can't tell the truth about how I feel.

Have to protect everybody else.
Can't be myself.
Can't hesitate. *Have* to act.
Can't ever truly, fully,
be alive.

INDEX

ABOUT THE AUTHOR

Since 1993, Ian Brennan has lectured over 1,000 hours per year and has successfully trained tens of thousands of people internationally in violence prevention and conflict resolution at shelters, schools, hospitals, clinics, jails, and addiction treatment programs, including such prestigious organizations as the Betty Ford Center, Bellevue Hospital, and Stanford University. These trainings are based on his over 15 years of experience working as a mental health specialist in locked, acute psychiatric settings, the job that has been rated as "the most dangerous" for assault in the state of California.

He also consults throughout the United States, providing one-on-one anger management sessions for individuals facing criminal charges due to violent conduct, and regularly provides expert testimony in such cases.

Additionally, he has produced two GRAMMY®-nominated records as well as musical projects with artists such as Merle Haggard, Green Day, Fugazi, filmmaker John Waters, and many more.

He was born and raised in the San Francisco Bay Area and currently lives abroad.

ViolencePrevention.us